The Kid from
Simcoe Street

The Kid *from* Simcoe Street

A Memoir and Poems

JAMES CLARKE

Introduction by
The Honourable R. Roy McMurtry

Poetry Editor
Bruce Meyer

Library and Archives Canada Cataloguing in Publication

Clarke, James
    The kid from Simcoe Street : a memoir and poems / James Clarke ;
introduction by R. Roy McMurtry ; poetry editor, Bruce Meyer.

ISBN 978-1-55096-260-4

    1. Clarke, James. 2. Poets, Canadian (English)--21st century--Biography.
3. Judges--Ontario--Biography. I. Meyer, Bruce, 1957- II. Title.

PS8555.L37486Z464 2012   C811'.54   C2012-902639-5

Design and Composition by Thank Heaven for Little Boys~mc
Typeset in Fairfield at the Moons of Jupiter Studios
Printed by Imprimerie Gauvin

Published by Exile Editions Ltd ~ www.ExileEditions.com
144483 Southgate Road 14 – GD, Holstein, Ontario, N0G 2A0
Printed and Bound in Canada in 2012

The publisher would like to acknowledge the financial support of the Canada
Council for the Arts, the Government of Canada through the Canada Book
Fund (CBF), the Ontario Arts Council, and the Ontario Media Development
Corporation, for our publishing activities.

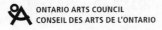

Canadian Sales: The Canadian Manda Group, 165 Dufferin Street,
Toronto ON M6K 3H6   www.mandagroup.com   416 516 0911

North American and international Distribution, and U.S. Sales:
Independent Publishers Group, 814 North Franklin Street,
Chicago IL 60610   www.ipgbook.com   toll free: 1 800 888 4741

For my parents.

I am also indebted to my friends and editors, Kevin Burns and Barry Callaghan, for their encouragement and editorial assistance. My special gratitude to Bruce Meyer for his creative selection of my poems, and to the Honourable R. Roy McMurtry for his introduction.

To Kathy, my wife, my deep gratitude for her patience and insights during the emotional ups and downs of my re-entry into the past.

CONTENTS

Part Two

THE WAR THAT NEVER ENDED

Part Three

FLYING HOME THROUGH THE DARK

SELECTED POEMS

Some names, circumstances and time sequences have been changed to preserve privacy and give the narrative dramatic shape. This is a memoir, not an autobiography, a snapshot of one period of my life as I remember it. There is no authorized version of a shared past.

In another life, this place was my home.
I feel the rising of a forgotten knowledge
like a spring from hidden aquifers under the earth.

—SUSAN MUSGRAVE, "Obituary of Light"

Introduction

by the Honourable R. Roy McMurtry

I am pleased to have been invited to write an introduction to the memoir of James Clarke, whom I have had the pleasure of knowing for many years as an accomplished lawyer, distinguished judge and as a published and respected poet. This memoir deals with a period of Jim's life beginning with his early childhood in Peterborough, Ontario, and his departure for McGill University.

The book also contains a section of his poetry, as selected by Bruce Meyer. Professor Meyer, as the reader will discover, appropriately describes James Clarke as "a brilliant poet who knows how to harness powerful ideas that seldom come easy or without great cost." He also refers to "the necessity of love and dignity and empathy and mercy and wisdom" that resides at the core of Clarke's work.

The combination of the tale of Jim's early life and the "editing" of his poems provides a powerful and moving experience for the reader.

James Clarke narrates a remarkable story of his early years. It is written with candour, passion, eloquence and integrity. He displays an incredible memory which describes his youth in great detail. He grew up in a largely dysfunctional and relatively poor family, with an alcoholic father, and a loving but sometimes alcoholic mother. However, he also shared his early life with two obviously fine and caring sisters who added an important dimension to his life.

James Clarke's descriptions of his father are incredibly poignant but in no way hateful. Passages about his father are powerfully and eloquently written. The following sentences, which I found very moving, are but an illustration of his prose poetry:

"Dad and I had lost each other in the shadow of each other's silences. Dad, another child in the house, never did learn the language of touch. He spurned embraces and other displays of affection. It was as if after his experiences of war he had built a box and, gathering all his hurts and silences, had curled up inside it like a shivering dog, leaving us to peer through the slats to glimpse his face in blades of light, to listen to the slow shrivelling of his heart."

"I believe that Dad's drinking was also a form of slow suicide, a deliberate shutting out of the past and a foreclosure of the future, the only way he knew to cope with the pain of daily living."

For me, these passages and many others are a most memorable and hugely eloquent description of pain in its most human dimensions.

The principal and important message in this memoir is how a young man, through force of character and intelligence, emerged from seemingly insurmountable odds to become a successful lawyer and distinguished judge of the Ontario Superior Court of Justice. James Clarke emerges from his youth as a man who understands how bad things happen to good people, how good people should not be intimidated by the dark realities of life, and how good people should demonstrate sympathy for the underdog and the afflicted. His poetry reflects the human face of law.

While it is not part of his memoir, the reader should know that he graduated from McGill University in 1956, attended Osgoode Hall Law School, and was then called to the Bar. Shortly after his marriage, he moved to Cobourg where he raised a family of seven children.

In 1968-69 he took a sabbatical and went to France with his wife and children to work with Jean Vanier at L'Arche with the mentally and physically disabled. The experience led to his first book, *L'Arche Journal*, published by Griffin House, Toronto, in 1973.

James Clarke was appointed to what is now the Superior Court of Justice in 1983. I became the Associate and Chief Justice of that court beginning in 1991, and had the privilege of working with him in that court until 1996. I soon became aware of his compassion as a judge. Our paths continued to intersect during the years 1996 to 2007 when I served as Chief Justice of Ontario.

A huge personal disaster occurred to Jim when his first wife, Mary, jumped to her death over Niagara Falls on April 8, 1990. Her body was never found. This absolutely devastating tragedy "collapsed the foundation" of his existence. He experienced an immense struggle to come to terms with what had happened.

In 1995, visiting in the Laurentians, James Clarke wrote his first poems. Many others soon followed. To quote Jim: "it was as if a dam burst releasing years of pent-up feelings, painful childhood memories, unhealed adolescent wounds all intermingled with the sharp debris of bereavement..."

Susan Musgrave, the well-known Canadian poet, learned of his poetry and found him the distinguished publisher and writer, Barry Callaghan. His first book of poetry, *Silver Mercies,* was published in 1997, and seven more collections rapidly followed. In Jim's words, "Mary's suicide was an axe breaking the frozen seas within me."

In his essay, "Swervings of the Heart," James Clarke wrote about his poetry and the fact that judging others left "little room for literary imagination and intuition." In the same essay he said:

"In my metamorphosis from judge to 'poet judge',
I came to see more clearly that we are all on a
common journey toward death and that all human
judgments are, at best, one-sided and incomplete."

"There are fields beyond ideas of right doing and wrong doing / where the soul can lie down among wildflowers / and lack nothing...."

James Clarke has truly lived and continues to live a remarkable life. He has learned and found growth out of a human tragedy. His poetry was obviously nurtured by his concerns for the poor, the disadvantaged and the afflicted. His creative genius will continue to inspire and entertain.

The two QR codes within the text, or accessed via the URLs below, link to short videos featuring the author speaking in relation to the introduction:

"The Human Face of Law" ~ 2:30
www.tinyurl.com/KidSimcoeStreet-HumanFace

"A Suicide Opened the Door" ~ 1:58
ww.tinyurl.com/KidSimcoeStreet-OnSuicide

Part One

FIRE HALL BOY

A TWO-STORIED, RED-BRICK TERRACE DIVIDED INTO THREE TENEMENTS

For the first 18 years of my life, 249 Simcoe Street was my precarious foothold in a world turning increasingly cold and hostile. As a child I had a powerful urge to locate myself, to affirm my place in the universe. As with most children, I was the centre of my own world and, like many, my school-books bore the inscription:

JAMES HENRY CLARKE
249 SIMCOE STREET
PETERBOROUGH
ONTARIO
CANADA
NORTH AMERICA
THE SOLAR SYSTEM
THE UNIVERSE

The downtown where we lived was a few city blocks bounded by George Street on the east and Aylmer on the west. Almost anything you needed, from furniture and cars to groceries, was within walking distance, and groceries could be delivered to your doorstep free of charge. The CNR tracks ran along Bethune Street, only a few feet from our tenement. The train would start up at the old station a block away, and as it chugged forward the engine would hiss, the large piston rods churning faster and faster as the train rumbled through our intersection, clanging and belching clouds of steam, the slatted railway cars rattling. I loved to stand beside the tracks and listen to the four blast whistles (long, long, short, long) warning drivers to stay clear of the intersection, and allow the acrid-smelling steam to envelop me, lost in billows of cindery smoke, powerful and invisible like my radio hero, Lamont Cranston in *The Shadow*. In the dead of night, the thunder of the freight cars shook the floorboards of the tenement, rattled the walls and rocked my bed. I pictured the orange glow on the sweaty faces of the firemen shovelling coal into the belly of the beast. Sometimes, I'd hitch a ride on a side ladder of the evening train and hang on for a block or two before jumping off.

Home was a two-storied, red-brick terrace divided into three tenements, ours in the middle. Built before Confederation, the window frames were askew and fissures gaped in the flaking brickwork. Each tenement had a rusty tin-roofed shed and a small dandelion-choked yard at the back, surrounded by a dilapidated wooden fence.

Mom's clothesline teetered across the yard. Before the York Trading Company bought the land beyond the fence, it belonged to Nelson's Coal and Lumber Company, and the air reeked of coal dust.

Simcoe Street was cruel to beauty. Each time Mom planted flowers in the earthen strip in front of the tenement, the blooms and the low green metal fence she erected to shield them would get trampled flat. Even the canopy of soft green lace the elms at the corner of Aylmer and Simcoe made in the spring didn't last.

I had a recurrent dream about the yellow fire hydrant in the boulevard in front of the tenement. In my dream, water was always gushing out its sides, flushing sidewalk, street and gutters clean of grit and grime, bestowing a lustrous red sheen on the battered tin fence of Pinkus's scrap yard across the street.

The front door opened into a dark hallway with a large kitchen at the end. Off the hallway on the left, as you entered, was Mom and Dad's bedroom, and on the right a small parlour where an upright piano stood under a coloured portrait of a gentle-looking Jesus with pierced feet holding his bleeding heart. Next to the kitchen was an unheated room we called the summer kitchen, with an unpainted, splintery wood floor, which served as a laundry room and general storeroom. A trap door in the floor at one end of the room, with an embedded metal ring you had to pull to lift, led down a rickety stairway to an earthen cellar lit by a single naked bulb. In its dank and dark recesses Mom stored her preserves on shelves, and one time she trapped a rat the size of rabbit at the open end of a broken sewer pipe near the front wall.

Three drafty bedrooms and a small bathroom comprised the upstairs.

After the war, Dad brought home a large wood panel from the bar at the Empress that the hotel had thrown out, on which a journeyman artist had depicted in oils a lake scene in the Rockies, and hung it upstairs in the hall beside my bedroom. I was starved for beauty and the painting enthralled me. I loved to trace my fingers over the hard edges of the paint, the ridges of snow-capped mountains, pines, cattails, and shoreline, marvelling at the wizardry of the unknown artist.

The tenement had no furnace, only a wood stove in the kitchen and a potbelly coal stove in the parlour, with a stovepipe suspended by wires that ran upstairs through a hole in the ceiling. Freezing winter mornings, my breath appeared in puffs of white vapour and I'd snuggle under the blankets, blinking in my pyjamas, dim-witted from sleep, to stay warm till Mom or Dad fired the stoves. The lacework of frost on the windowpane captivated me. Though it shot cold shivers through every nerve of my body and made me wince, I loved to scrape my fingernails across its exotic ferns and flowers.

Dad considered our tenement a castle; Mom called it a pigsty. Mom was the chief breadwinner; Dad only allotted half his earnings to the household. She'd make invidious comparisons to the "nice detached home" that Tommy Kingdom had bought for her sister Marie on Stewart Street, a few blocks away. Dad was impervious to her pleading. Extending his hands like Moses, he'd proclaim, "Ach, go on

with you, Florie. We've got everything we need right here."
To which she'd reply, "This place is no Buckingham Palace,
no matter what you think, Sammy."

Simcoe Street offered myriad diversions to fire a boy's
imagination. It was there I got my first inkling of the power
of music. The chords of Mantovani's rendition of the tradi-
tional English folk song "Greensleeves," which came undu-
lating over the airwaves regularly Sunday evenings, moved
me to tears, untied the knot of anger inside me.

Not only was the tenement close to the three movie the-
atres downtown – the Regent, the New Centre and the
Capital – the neighbourhood embraced a fire hall, the rail-
way station, a Salvation Army temple, a synagogue, a
Chinese hand laundry, and three scrap yards. Pinkus's yard
across the street, piled high with used car parts, twisted
pipes, old boilers, rusty girders, large flat slabs of steel
slurred with rust, and mountains of old magazines and yel-
lowing newspapers, which reeked of damp and decay, lured
us to wiggle through its wooden gates to play war games,
cops and robbers, hide-and-seek among the heaps of junk.
The jaws of the giant metal cutter held me in awe; not even
the hardest metal could withstand its powerful bite. Sunday
summer evenings, the Salvation Army band would assem-
ble outside the temple up the street, and the sound of bas-
soons, cymbals, tambourines, horns, drums and trombones
reverberated through the soft twilight. And behind our ten-
ement rose the square brick tower of the fire hall where the
firemen dangled the wet hoses like spaghetti to dry. In the
deep-shadowed fold between day and night I'd hear the

muffled clang of horseshoes, see the firemen's cigarettes flare in the horseshoe pit at the side of the hall.

What I most vividly remember is the scrim of neon light after the war above the downtown skyline shimmering in the dark, the darkness alive with the hum and honk of traffic, snatches of laughter and conversation carried on the breeze and, occasionally, the faint bark of a dog or the wild lung of an ambulance. And most memorable of all, the *pee-ent, pee-ent* of the nighthawks in the inky sky. I'd hide under the blankets and listen to the thump, thump, thump of my heart, a beat so relentless and unwavering I imagined I was being stalked by a stranger, convinced that if he ever caught me my heart would stop forever.

A FADED POLAROID

I was the oldest child in the family and had two sisters, Shirl, and Marilyn, known as Babe, the youngest. Recently, I visited my sister Babe at her home in Mississauga. She sat beside a tall glass cabinet crammed with expensive designer dolls; there were so many the cabinet couldn't contain them all. They spilt out onto the floor and mantel. She must have noticed my puzzlement. Apologetically, she said, "As a child my greatest dream was to own a china doll, but Mom couldn't afford it."

She took a sip of coffee and after a long pause added, "You know, I don't have many good memories of Simcoe Street and I hardly remember Dad at all."

Babe is a big woman with a round open face and the strong bones of her "Norn Iron" ancestry, except for the eyes, which are large, blue and soft like Mom's. Her eyes began to tear up. "But I do remember the time just after the war when he got mad because I'd gone out with the Booth boy against his wishes. He'd taken off his belt to whack me and you stopped him, grabbed his arm and yelled, 'Touch her and I'll kill you.'"

"I don't remember that."

"You did, Jim, you did. And I remember the day we went to Jack Lundy's to choose his casket. Tears were running down Jack's cheeks and you said: 'You must have really loved my father' until Jack told you he had a defective tear duct and might have to have an operation.

"And the day of the funeral, remember?" she went on, "so hot and sunny."

"I thought it rained."

"It was hot and sunny, because none of us could stop laughing in the limousine as Dad's army buddies carried him out of the church, hot and sweating, and Dad's old drinking pal, Jack the undertaker, kept opening and shutting his mouth like a turtle, a sure sign he'd dried out and needed a quickie."

"The poor driver must have thought we were crazy, carrying on at our father's funeral like that," I said.

Babe's first marriage, which was unhappy, had ended in divorce. Her second husband was good to her, but had died young. She has two grown-up children who are close to her.

"I get angry when I think back to Simcoe Street," she said. "Gabby was a sicko. Today they'd have charged her for what she did."

Gabby was the housekeeper Mom hired to help take care of us during the war while Dad was overseas.

"She treated you and Shirl better than me," Babe went on, "and Shirl lapped it up, as if it was her right."

"For Pete's sake, Babe, Shirl's dead, let bygones be bygones," I said, surprised to hear myself repeating an expression Dad had always used when Mom got bitter and dredged up his past transgressions. As far as I can remember Shirl and Babe had had a love-hate relationship. Babe was obese and shy while Shirl was daring and loved the boys. In her teens, Shirl was one of the best jitterbuggers in the city, so good other dancers would clear the floor of the Brock Street Arena to watch her. Shirl, like Babe, married twice and had three children; two daughters by the first, and a boy by the second marriage. Tragically, her second husband also passed away prematurely at 55. Shirl died of cancer of the cervix in her mid-40s. Babe never got over it.

"She asked me to forgive her before she died," she said, her eyes moistening. "You didn't know that did you?"

"No."

"Well, it's true."

Shirl's death had walloped me, too. When I got the news at the cottage, the deck shimmied beneath me and I almost keeled over.

After a pause Babe said, "You owe me, too."

"What do you mean, owe you?"

"Well, you got all the breaks."

"What breaks?"

"You went to university and escaped," she said, "and now you're a judge."

"You could have escaped also, but chose to quit school," I reminded her. "Remember the nuns begging Mom to keep you in school? But you, pigheaded, refused."

"That doesn't matter, you still owe me," she said, a mischievous half-smile on her face.

"Okay, if it'll make you feel any better I'll take you out for dinner tonight," I said. "That'll do for now," she said. "But I'll choose the restaurant."

Babe brought out a large cardboard box of Mom's old photographs. We sifted through them for a long time and I picked out a faded Polaroid that someone had taken of Dad at work in a ditch on Aylmer Street when he was with Hydro; he's squinting at the camera, thick red hands cupped over the handle of a spade, a pile of earth in the background. He looks sweaty and ill at ease. To pedestrians, he could have been an old stump rooted in the earth. Dust covers his yellow hard hat, checked flannel shirt and baggy green work pants, erasing the sharp lines from his face. I showed Babe the photo. "He looks like a ghost."

We searched everywhere through piles of old Kodak shots but one picture was absent: we couldn't find a family photo of Mom, Dad, me, and my two sisters together. It doesn't exist.

Our conversation opened a tap inside me, led to a flood of forgotten memories. The week of Dad's death I'd gone on a fishing trip to my aunt Palma's lake in the High Laurentians, near Ste-Veronique. The morning after my arrival, I was observing Minoune, Palma's pregnant old yellow cat as she prepared to give birth in the screen porch. She lay down in a wooden box and rolled over on her side like she was about to nap. As five shiny sacs slid out, Minoune chewed through the umbilical cords, which were tough as old leather. By early afternoon, a mass of breathing fur clung to her belly. Then Palma punched holes in the bottom of a large yellow margarine container and filled a large pail with lukewarm water. After putting Minoune outside, she gently lifted the newborn kittens one by one and laid them in the yellow container. Then she lowered it into the pail. Placing the lid on the container, she set a stone on top. "I always say a little prayer before I do this," she said, glancing back as she descended the stairway to the basement. "They make my dahlias grow." The phone rang. It was Mom, she was sobbing.

"Your dad's dying," she said, "you'd better come home right away if you ever want to see him alive again."

All the way back I felt terrible that I had left so hastily and had not stayed with Mom and my sisters, the people I love, during Dad's last days. After a five-hour drive, I finally reached the hospital and spied Mom, bleary-eyed with grief, in the corridor outside Dad's room. I knew I'd arrived too late. "Your father passed away fifteen minutes ago," she said. We hugged each other in the corridor a long time.

When I entered Dad's room alone, the venetian blinds were half-closed, the room stuffy and eerily quiet. A beige plastic curtain surrounded the bed. I could hear the thumping of my heart. Guilt and regret roiled inside me. Mostly it was anger, anger at being absent when I was most needed, anger at the hospital for not saving his life, and especially anger at him.

All my life I'd been cheated of a father and now I'd been cheated by death. Who would I find behind the curtain? I tried to pray. I took a deep breath and yanked open the curtain. Yes, it was Dad, a husk of his former self, diminished, wasted, but him: gaunt and sharp-boned as though all the excess of his hard living and restless spirit had been removed, leaving a younger version of himself, a look of unshakable serenity – something he never possessed in life. I stroked his hands; they were still warm, but the skin was already beginning to cool. For a long time I gazed at this passionate Irishman who was my father, no longer flesh and blood, now an icon of clay, and felt a deep sadness for my mother, my sisters, and especially for him and me – for all the might-have-beens – the gulf we'd never been able to bridge. Later, at the Little Lake cemetery, as they lowered his coffin into the ground, I picked up a spade, dug into the pyramid of crumbling earth and scattered a few shovelfuls, the earth bouncing and rattling on the shiny top of the cas-. ket. Overwrought, I imagined the casket had no bottom, and I remembered the old gypsy saying: You have to dig deep to bury a father.

On a trip I recently made to Peterborough, my home-town, an emotional topography freighted with the sharp debris of the past also surged back. The day of the visit was gusty and wet; the streets lacquered with rain. The decrepit terrace on Simcoe Street, where for years our family had eked out a living, had been converted into a financial office dedicated to making your money grow. St. Peter's, my old school, had been razed to make room for condominiums, and a modern new city library now occupied the site of the fire hall where I'd spent so much of my youth. I was aston-ished how miniscule my childhood world now appeared, circumscribed by a few city streets. Everything seemed lost in transience, save for the Otonabee River that continued to flow slowly and majestically through the downtown as though time were its ally.

As I drove to the Little Lake cemetery that afternoon, I passed the site of Canada Packers (now a motel) on George Street, next to the Otonabee River where Dad had once taken me fishing, and recalled a poem I'd written:

Red suspenders gleaming
he stumbled over railway ties
and rancid wooden crates
behind the packing plant
as I tried to catch up.
'The fish won't wait," I heard him say
before he vanished.

I found him on the concrete bank
beneath the iron bridge
guzzling from a silver flask,
cursing the big, black suckers
swirling past.
I watched in silence till he
snapped the line and yelled:
'God damn!"
said we had to go.

All the way home I trailed
his wobbly legs.

Is it too late?

Will I ever catch him now?

I hadn't visited the cemetery since the interment and had forgotten where we'd laid him. For what seemed like hours I paced that autumn-stained precinct, bewildered by the maze of stones glistening in the greyness. After a while all the trees and markers began to look the same and I gave up, frustrated and exhausted. It was as if Dad had been cunningly mislaid, locked so deeply inside the dark cabinet of earth that no key or clue could find his hiding place.

Dad was like a stranger you meet in a fog, voice muffled, features blurred. It was as though the alcohol that consumed his life contained a secret potion that rendered him invisible. Or he was someone who went to war and never came back, missing in action. And then I remembered Babe's description during our visit. She's right; he is a ghost. And I'm still looking for his face.

GET MOVIN', YOU DOGANS,
OR YOU'LL BE LATE FOR MASS!

Dad was born into a working-class family in Belfast, Northern Ireland, on the 19th of July, 1909. His father operated a giant crane in the Harland and Wolff shipyards and Dad always claimed that his death was triggered by an electrical accident on the job.

Ireland had a long history of English domination, rebellion and sectarian violence. The failed Easter Rebellion of 1916 gave birth to a "terrible beauty," as Yeats phrased it, which eventually resulted in the establishment of the Irish Free State in 1922. But independence came at a high price: the British hived off the six counties in the north, known as Ulster, into a Protestant-dominated statelet that would remain part of the United Kingdom and outside the new Ireland that the North feared and despised.

The North, from which the Gaels had been driven in the 17th century to make room for Protestant, mostly Scottish, settlements known as the Ulster Plantation, became a simmering battleground between diehard nationalists who never gave up the dream of a united Ireland and the obdurate, "no-surrender" fundamentalist "Prods," as the Protestants were known, who maintained their ascendancy through systemic economic and political discrimination. Dad came from this tribe of hard, laconic men who hated Catholics and shouted, "What we have, we hold!" He was one of those who insisted on marching through Catholic neighbourhoods wearing bowler hats, while carrying rolled umbrellas, and orange sashes to the beat of giant battle drums. Their symbol was the bloody severed red hand.

Dad, who'd been baptized in the Protestant Church of Ireland (Anglican), was sent to Sunday school where he learned the names of every book of the Old Testament by rote, which he loved to recite at gatherings. His mother, Mary Elizabeth, was a teetotaller who abhorred smoking (an aversion Dad inherited). His army records indicate that he completed the equivalent of grade 9 in school. He always boasted he topped the class.

Mom later told me that Dad had been an avid reader. I remember *Prisoners All*, a collection of daring and ingenious escape stories by British prisoners during the First Great War. The detailed maps of the various German camps, with their miniscule x's for barbed wire and small dots for sentries and larger ones for machine-gun emplacements, mesmerized me. Dad had lost his eldest brother, Willie, in that conflict.

The Salvation Army sponsored him to come to Canada as an indentured farm boy under a scheme (later known as the Golden Bridge) that promoted sending abroad to various English-speaking Commonwealth countries young men and women of "good British stock" who, for chiefly economic reasons, had no future in their own country.

Dad's mother, widowed for a second time when he was 13 (Dad claimed he woke up in bed with his dead father's cold feet pressed against his cheek), was left with seven mouths to feed on the modest salary of a doffing mistress in a Belfast linen factory. She must have regarded Canada both as an opportunity for Dad to break away from the mean streets of Belfast and a way of relieving her own dire poverty. All his life Dad retained a soft spot for the Sally Ann and its work.

On the first day of February in 1926, Dad, then 16 years old, sailed from Liverpool to Halifax on the 14,080-ton Cunard passenger ship *Alunia*, and reached his final destination by rail, a farm in Bobcaygeon, Ontario, belonging to the Thompson family, straight-laced, industrious, church-going folk who neither drank nor smoked.

Decades later, when I was a young lawyer in Cobourg and had a small branch office in Bobcaygeon, Mr. Thompson, the patriarch of the family, then a widower, came to my office and told me that on the evening of Dad's arrival he and his wife had gone to the local station to fetch him, but he was nowhere to be seen. The conductor suggested that they search the entire train. They found him in the last coach, curled up on a seat, clutching his battered brown suitcase, face streaked with tears.

Mr. Thompson said Dad was a good worker and after three years, when he decided to take a job as bellhop at the Empress Hotel in Peterborough, Mr. Thompson was sorry to see him go.

"He'd become like a son to us," he said, "and we didn't think the hotel was a good place for him." Though Dad was loyal to his Ulster roots (portraits of his mother and siblings adorned our parlour walls for years) he always referred to the Thompsons as "Ma and Pa."

Mom came from an old French-Canadian family of Norman lineage with roots in Canada going back to the 17th century. She'd been born with a quick mind, and her father had enrolled her in a one-room English-speaking school in the Eastern Townships, where she'd excelled and became fluent in English. The Depression drove her to Ontario, at age 17, to find work as a domestic. After various jobs, she finally landed a position in Peterborough as a waitress at the Empress Hotel, which possessed the finest dining room in the city. She met Dad, who by then was holding down two jobs: bellhop and switchboard operator.

I've seen early photos of her; she was petite and attractive, with soft creamy skin, wavy auburn hair and large blue eyes. Raised on a farm, she had an abiding love of nature and the outdoors. She was also very athletic and, for a period in the 1930s, she had been one of the city's champion bowlers.

In the 1930s and 1940s, the Catholic Church frowned upon mixed marriages. A non-Catholic who wished to marry a Catholic had to covenant in writing that any children of the marriage would be raised in the One True Apostolic Faith.

Mom and Dad were married in the rectory of St. Peter's Cathedral in 1932 and I was born on December 14th 1933, followed by my sister Shirley (Shirl) in 1935 and my sister Marilyn (Babe) the following year. The year of my birth was inauspicious. Unknown to me, Hitler was elected Chancellor of Germany and my doom-proof world of childhood was about to crumble as the world began to bumble toward disaster.

Days after I was born, Dad had second thoughts about his commitment. As Mom recounted the story, he announced out of the blue that Canon Robertson would be presiding over my baptism the following Sunday in St. John's Anglican Church. The sponsors were already chosen, he informed her, and he'd made arrangements for a small celebration at the house afterwards. His change of heart stunned her.

"How could you go back on your word, Sam?" she implored, teary-eyed.

"No son of mine will ever be raised a Taig," he declared.

Neither tears nor anything she said would dissuade him. Stung by his betrayal, she immediately threw on her woollen winter coat and rushed off to see Father Finn at St. Peter's. Father Finn listened to her distraught story and afterwards reflected for a long time. Then he unveiled his solution. "Get two Catholic sponsors and bring the boy to the church Friday night and we'll baptize him first," he said. "It's the first baptism that counts, Mrs. Clarke. Another one won't do the boy any lasting harm." He also suggested that she say nothing to Dad. "Family peace is a precious gift," he said.

Thus I was christened in two major branches of the Christian faith the same week. As for Dad's broken promise, only later, when the time came for me to enroll in separate school, did he learn what had happened. But by then it was too late. The second Battle of the Boyne was over.

Mom had been engaged twice before she met Dad. Her second fiancé was an Englishman, who would later become one of the top executives at General Motors in Oshawa. Years later, after disillusionment with Dad had set in, I asked her if she ever regretted leaving him for Dad.

"I wasn't in love with that man," she said. "I fell in love with your father. I guess I couldn't resist that big dimple in his chin. And in those days he was a smart dresser and didn't drink much."

While Mom and Dad were outsiders in Ontario, they were opposites in background. Though neither attended church regularly, each wore their religion as a tribal badge of identity. Dad had inherited a "black, Protestant upbringing" as Mom described it, which left him with an almost visceral distaste for anything faintly "Romanish" and a propensity to crack jokes about the Pope's nose. Mom was intransigently Catholic. Yet, later on, it was Dad, not Mom, who would, on Sunday mornings, stand at the foot of the stairs and bellow at me and my two sisters: "Get movin', you dogans, or you'll be late for Mass!" and, if we didn't move promptly, he'd march up the stairs and hammer on the bedroom doors till we got out of bed.

A Presbyterian at heart, he disapproved of profanity and smutty language, and woe betide anyone who uttered a sexual innuendo in his presence. Even when he was half-snapped, I recall him muttering his night prayers beside his bed, sometimes dozing off on his knees.

There is an old photo of Mom in Chemong, standing on an old wooden floating bridge, the world's longest – 2,628 feet straight across the lake – a shaky structure rigged together with iron bars, chains and boulders. Mom is gazing across the lake, a look of sadness on her face. She seems hardly conscious of me, snuggled in her arms. Years later, my sister Babe told me that this photo was taken the day she learned of his first betrayal. After that disillusionment, I suspect Mom diverted some of her affection onto me, the outgoing Gerber baby, whom passersby would stop to look at with clucking admiration for, and by all accounts, I became the apple of her eye.

Mom told me Dad knew how to flash on the Irish charm and travellers loved him. He'd greet them at the revolving front doors of the hotel with his blarney smile and a hearty handshake. Then he'd tote their luggage up the winding oak stairs to the darkly varnished rooms, regaling them with the latest news. Always accommodating and keen to please, he'd fetch them bootleg liquor. They were unanimous in their opinion: "A good fella," they'd say, tipping him handsomely. "A prince on the street, a devil at home," was Mom's wry commentary.

When Mom went on like this about Dad, I would wonder with a tinge of sadness what it would have been like to have met him for the first time, to feel the clasp of his hand, and hear him say just once, "If there's anything you need, Jim, just ask."

LATER, I PROMISE

We are at Chemong Lake for a picnic. Dad wants to take me for a swim on his back, but I am fearful and shake my head. Mom tells me not worry, Dad's a strong swimmer, I'll be safe, but her words bring little consolation. I am on the verge of tears and begin to shake. Dad is insistent, orders me to climb his back, wrap my arms around his neck and hang on tight. I do what I'm told. Dad's back feels massive, clammy and slippery. As he breast strokes away from the beach my fears mount and I begin to sob, but after a while, when I realize I am safe and am not going to fall off and drown, I calm down and begin to enjoy the ride. We circle in the water for a few minutes and then Dad heads back to shore.

"That was fun, aye, Jimmy," he says afterwards. "We'll do it again." Later, when I ask for another ride, he's drinking and waves me off. "Not now, lad," he says. "Later, I promise." But he doesn't keep his promise.

Mom is making apple pies in the kitchen and the room is filled with the fragrance of fresh-cut apples. Outside, the sun is blazing, morning sunlight has swept clear the sky.

"Why don't you go out and play, Jim," she says.

I gather up my trucks and step into the dazzle of the August day. The air shimmers with whirring and thrumming insects. I slip into the York Trading yard through a gap in the fence and plunk myself down in the shady canyon of the driveway between the tenement and the York Trading building. The earth feels cool under my bottom as I run my trucks over the smooth flat rocks embedded in the driveway. Suddenly, I hear the crunch of tires and glance up to see a monster of steel and glass rolling toward me. The monster stops just as Mom rushes out of the tenement and a burly red-faced man hops from the cab, hollering, "For Chrissakes, kid! You coulda got killed!" I burst into tears as Mom sweeps me up in her arms and whisks me into the tenement.

She rocks me a long time in the parlour. When my sobbing subsides she grips my shoulder, tears in her eyes: "You must never, never play in the driveway ever again," she says. Then she hugs me again so hard I can feel her heart pounding. "I love you so much," she says.

I'm four or five, standing in the hallway near the kitchen door. A party is in progress, fiery words are spoken, and Mom pours Dad's liquor into the kitchen sink. Through a shroud of blue smoke I see Dad punch Mom in the face, watch in horror as blood spouts from her nose, splattering her white blouse and the linoleum. I become hysterical, scream over and over, "Stop! Stop! Stop!" but no one pays attention. Palma, Mom's youngest sister who is staying with us, grabs Mom's favourite white porcelain swan from the hallway table and crashes it down on Dad's head, drawing blood and bringing an abrupt end to the fight. Later, Mom comes to my room where I'm cowering under the blankets, still sobbing. Wads of bloodied Kleenex protrude from her nostrils, a sight I can't bear to look at. Mom's hand smooths my brow. Dad didn't mean it; it was the drink that did it, she tells me. I'm inconsolable. For weeks afterwards I can't get Mom's screams and blood out of my head.

I'm alone with Mom in the kitchen on Simcoe Street. She's getting ready for work, ironing her uniform. I'm sitting by the window, dazzled by the geometric shapes the slanting sun is making on the linoleum. Except for the soft clunk of the iron on the board and the crackle of the wood stove, a stillness fills the kitchen. I feel an oozing sensation under my thighs and reach into my shorts. I'm about to bring the stinky brown substance to my lips when Mom shrieks, "*Merde*, Jim, *merde, merde!*" slams down the iron, rushes me over to the sink, muttering, "Bad, bad, bad," as she scrubs out my mouth with soap and water. Horrified, I'm convinced I've just poisoned myself and will soon die. A couple of months later Mom is bathing me in the galvanized tub on the kitchen table when her friend Trixie and her daughter Gloria arrive. I twist my four-year-old naked body to face them, hands clamped behind my bottom, deathly afraid they'll see the source of my secret shame.

I'm standing on a mahogany bar in a smoky beer parlour, bare knees clamped together, staring at the brown moons of Dad's eyes far below. "Can't you see the boy's scared, Sam?" one of his cronies says as the others laugh. "No son of mine's a coward," he shouts, moons shrinking to crescents. "Jump, you Fenian, jump!" And so I do what I'm told, close my eyes, and jump into his unsteady arms.

DAD WAS LUCKY THAT DAY

The Great Depression of the Thirties hit Peterborough hard. In a decade of breadlines, panhandling and hobo jungles, no one was spared, but luckily Mom and Dad remained employed at the hotel and escaped its worst ravages. Our tenement became a port of call for a straggle of hungry down-and-outers, mostly unemployed young men who rode the rods to relieve the financial burden on their families; young men begging for bread, carrots or a few potatoes to take back to the hobo campsite in a ravine not far from the entrance to Jackson's Park where they huddled in front of their fires.

I recall Mom doling platefuls of *Pouding du Chomeur*, a cake concoction topped with sugar and boiling water. She handed out so many sandwiches to raggedy looking strangers that Dad began to harp, "You'll be putting us in the poor house, Florie," to which she'd reply, "We're already there, Sam."

Illicit gambling was rife in Peterborough in those years and Dad was addicted to craps, poker and horses. I remember hearing the strange incantations of Dad and his cronies shooting craps in the front parlour. Before throwing the dice, Dad would set his mom's portrait against the piano leg to bring him luck. It rarely did. Martin O'Sullivan ("Young Irish," as he was dubbed) from across the street ran a floating crap game, moving from safe house to safe house one step ahead of the law. I'd often see scraps of paper floating around the house with such baffling monikers as Lickity Split, Count Fleet, Quick and Easy, and Bullet Train. One time I fished a list from Dad's jacket and brought it to Mom to ask her what the names meant and she got furious. "What are you doing with your dad's things?" she snapped, grabbing the paper and tossing it in the kitchen stove. "Your father's been at the bookmaker's again, betting on horses," she added testily. One time he came home from an all-night session of poker dead broke. A heated argument in the kitchen ended in tears, Mom grumbling that Dad's gambling was sabotaging her dream of a new house.

One sunny Sunday, the year I turned six, Dad told me he was taking me on a picnic to Jackson's Park. Mom got me dressed up for the occasion – peaked cap, short pants, jacket, and knee socks – and fixed us a picnic basket. Later, Myles Gorman, Dad's drinking buddy, showed up in his Chevrolet to drive us to the park. I remember entering what looked like a greenhouse surrounded by dozens of parked cars and a crowd of boisterous men milling inside, drinking and shooting craps, some on one knee, blowing on dice and mouthing strange words, "boxcars," "snake eyes," etc., a lingo I didn't understand. I saw a man take off his shoes and shake the dice next to his ear before rolling them.

As the afternoon unfolded, I lost sight of Dad and Myles. I began to panic. I waded through a thicket of legs.

Out of a clear sky, what sounded like a school bell rang out and Dad, with Myles, materialized out of nowhere, grabbed me by the hand. "Hurry, Jimmy, we've got to go." We hustled out of the greenhouse to the parked car to make a quick exit from the park. Myles' white knuckles gripped the wheel. No one spoke as we drove straight home.

That evening I was in my room and heard Mom in the kitchen through the stovepipe hole scolding Dad. "How could you have been so stupid?" Years later, she told me that as we were making our exit the OPP anti-gambling squad was filtering through the trees of the park to make arrests. Many men had been charged that afternoon, including Young Irish, who got thirty days in the hoosegow. "Your dad was lucky that day," Mom sighed.

HERO

The fire hall was next door to the tenement. The scream of the sirens thrilled me. I loved to watch the firemen sliding down the brass poles, scrambling to put on their high boots and knee-length canvas coats heavy as sheepskins (these were the days before Nomex and Kevlar), hopping onto the tailboards of the pumpers after a fire call.

Throughout the city, fire alarm boxes were posted, each with a separate number. When an alarm was pulled the call was transmitted to the station, and the number of the box punched out in the coop with a loud clack-clacking noise telling the firemen where the blaze was located. After the men returned from a call, I'd watch them string up the wet hoses by their necks in the hose tower. The dripping hoses formed huge puddles on the concrete floor at the base of the tower, which always smelt mouldy and damp. I loved the rough, gritty feel of the hoses on my skin.

One day when I was five or six, I was in the York Trading yard playing marbles when I glanced up to see thick black smoke and sparks spewing out of our neighbour's chimney where Maggie James and her boarder, Jack Buller, lived. Alarmed, I raced to the fire hall to report what I'd seen.

Although the fire turned out to be minor and was quickly extinguished, news of my prompt action soon spread and I became a local hero on our street. Mom bought me a double chocolate cone, told me how proud I'd made her. Even Dad paid me a rare compliment. "You done good, lad," he said.

Maggie, our next-door neighbour, rewarded me with almond cookies. A day or two later, summoned to the fire hall, a newsman snapped a picture of Chief Virgil Frazer shaking my hand, congratulating me on my quick thinking.

"If it hadn't been for you, young man," Virgil said, "we might have had a major fire on our hands." The headline in the *Examiner* read: BOY REPORTS TIMNEY FIRE.

In those days, fire departments were male enclaves. Nothing enlivened my days more than to hang out at the station and learn the men's routines or to play checkers or pool with them in the upstairs lounge. Frequently, they'd commission me to run errands for them to Connell's, the corner store, to pick up soft drinks, chocolate bars, and sundry treats. The Chief was an imposing man with silky white hair, bushy white eyebrows and commanding light-blue eyes.

A veteran of the Great War who'd been wounded at Vimy Ridge, he ran the department like a military operation. The department had two daily shifts, a 56-hour work week on a six-day cycle, and every morning at 8 a.m. the men assembled in the fire hall yard like soldiers on parade. The chief grew fond of me and during the roll call he often allowed me to take part by standing beside him. He also had a private car, a Ford coupe, painted fire-engine red with "FIRE CHIEF" blazoned in yellow letters on the front doors, and sometimes he'd let me sit behind the wheel in the cab and pretend to drive. Occasionally, I'd ride with him on a fire call. Once, he took me to the George Street pier where the men were testing hoses, the silvery cascades of water jetting into Little Lake.

A year or so after the chimney fire, the Chief summoned me to the station and announced he was making it official: he had appointed me Fire Mascot for the department. "You've earned your stripes, young man," he said, reaching behind his desk and handing me a pint-sized waterproof turnout coat and a red British steel helmet, Deputy Chief PFD painted in large white letters on the front. One of my earliest ambitions was to become a fire chief like Virgil Frazer.

After my appointment, the Chief entrusted me with my first mission: finding a hidey-hole for his liquor in the hose tower. Whenever he needed a pick-me-up he'd give me a wink or a tug of his snow-white mane and I'd scoot upstairs, open the small low door into the tower and fetch his bottle from its hiding place, which I'd bring to him wrapped under a towel or newspaper. After he'd taken a good pull, it was my duty to return the bottle to its hidey-hole in the tower. I soon discovered that some of the other men were tippling in their parked cars behind the station from flat amber mickeys they'd stashed in glove compartments or under seats. News of my covert operation must have gotten around for, after a while, a few of them enlisted me to find nooks or crannies in that monstrous old building for their hooch, too.

Did these men drink because they were bored out of their skulls, I've often asked myself looking back. Were they knowingly or unknowingly exploiting me? In that more innocent age, the concept of child abuse, sexual or otherwise, never entered anyone's mind. The shared mission of saving lives and property from the ravages of fire bonded me to the men and made me feel, as fire mascot, that I was doing something noble and important.

In time, the fire hall was to become my sanctuary and an antidote for the loneliness I felt when Dad went overseas. I remember helping polish the brass and nickel fittings on the pumpers, waxing the dark oak floors of the cavernous hall till they gleamed. But mostly it's the quiet moments I recall – the firemen in the cool of the evening, shirt sleeves rolled up, digging in the flower garden they'd created behind the hall, moving nimbly between the rows of asters, cosmos, geraniums and tulips, or lounging about in the horseshoe pit in their blue shirts, small bow ties, and navy-blue trousers and peaked caps, almost invisible in the ebbing light as they whispered in the stillness of the evening.

DILEAS GU BAS

When Britain and Canada declared war on Germany in September 1939, Dad's brothers, like most loyal Ulstermen, quickly joined up. Danny, who had been a soldier in India before the war, was a member of the British Expeditionary Force (BEF). His younger brother, John, enlisted in the British Merchant Navy. Dad's Irish combative streak was aroused and he closely followed the German campaign in the newspapers as it blitzed across Poland, Denmark, Norway, and then the Netherlands, Belgium and France.

On May 10th, 1940, Nazi airpower spearheaded a fierce thrust through the Ardennes. Ill-prepared and demoralized, the Allied armies broke apart. During the evacuation of the BEF at Dunkirk, Danny was captured and spent the rest of the war as a prisoner of war in Germany. Danny's capture disturbed Dad deeply.

"A brave lad, Danny," he'd say, tears in his eyes. With typical cock-of-the-north bravado he put up a front, talked as though he could hardly wait to enter the fray, teach the Boche a lesson. Then, on the 28th of June, 1940, he came home from the hotel, tanked up, and launched his own lightning strike. He announced that he had enlisted that afternoon with the Stormont, Dundas, Glengarry Highlanders (SD and Gs), an infantry regiment from Cornwall that was recruiting in the Peterborough area. "I can't stand idly by while Britain fights for her life," he proclaimed.

Mom was devastated. A French Canadian, she had little sympathy for what she believed was a British imperial war on remote foreign shores. "How could you, Sam?" she demanded, sobbing. "You might be killed, the children don't deserve a dead father." His enlistment was to become a festering sore, an addition to her fattening file of grievances.

Dad was 30 years old when he volunteered in the SD and Gs, a regiment with a storied history going back to the 19th century. It was said of the regiment that it never failed to take an objective, never lost a yard of ground and never lost a man taken prisoner in offensive action. Its motto was: *Dileas Gu Bas* (Faithful Unto Death). The SD and Gs became part of the 9th Brigade, Third Canadian Division that landed on Juno Beach, Bernieres-sur-mer, on D-Day.

As a married man with young children, Dad could have sat out the war with honour. But no amount of pleading could change his mind. "Ulstermen aren't cowards," became his stubborn refrain.

Mom always maintained that it was boredom, not patriotism that had spurred him to volunteer. "He just wanted to escape the responsibilities of family life, that's it," she'd say.

The German menace seemed so scary I'd lie awake in my bed at night, ear pressed against the pillow, listening to the thump, thump, thump of my heartbeat, waiting to hear the tramp of boots on the staircase, convinced that Gestapo spies were stalking me and that they would strike at any moment.

Knowing that Dad would be soon shipped overseas, Mom decided she needed help and, on the recommendation of her sister Cecile who lived in Sherbrooke, Quebec, she hired Gabrielle Plante (we nicknamed her Gabby) as a full-time housekeeper. Cecile had gone to school with Gabby and knew her family, who owned a small electrical repair shop in Lennoxville, just outside Sherbrooke. Gabby was on the rebound after an unrequited love affair with a married man (I recall years later my mother hinting that she'd had a backstreet abortion), and wanted a change of scene. In her letter of recommendation Cecile said that Gabby was hardworking, an excellent cook and house-keeper, and that because of her disciplined and orderly character would be a good influence on us, the children.

Early that fall, Gabby arrived at our doorstep with two large suitcases and a small, black female mutt with floppy ears and a pointed muzzle that she called Cherie. Gabby was a slim, wiry woman, about Mom's age, with eyes dark as rivets and glistening raven hair that fell in curls to her shoulders. She had perfect eggshell-smooth skin; the sharp sculpted contours of her face gave her a bird-of-prey look. She had two rows of perfect white teeth, and several pro-nounced tics. Sometimes her head would jerk back and her mouth would twitch when she spoke and she'd often shrug and emit a bark-like yelp. She wasn't in the house five minutes that day before she asked if I would mind her dog.

"And be careful, Jeem," she said, handing me a leash. "I never let Cherie loose, especially near roads."

When we were alone I asked Mom about Gabby's tics.

"She was born that way," was all Mom said.

I learned that Gabby's condition was the result of a genetic misfire, an inherited neuropsychiatric disorder called Tourette's that is characterized by multiple motor and verbal tics. But I knew none of this and as a child regarded her tics as merely bizarre.

A boot camp consisting of a cavernous drill hall, a parade square and barracks had been hastily constructed at Lansdowne Exhibition Park in the south end of the city, where Dad underwent basic training for two months together with 800 to 1,000 other volunteers from all parts of Canada.

At first, the fledgling regiment drilled with broom handles, pith helmets, white shirts and civilian trousers. Sometimes they'd march in the city streets and I would race along the sidewalks trying to keep up with them. For me, war was a big adventure and I would brag to my friends about my father the soldier. I still have a black-and-white snap of him taken in Central Park. He appears slightly obese as he squints into the camera in his white shirt and trousers, with pith helmet and wide suspenders. He doesn't look like a soldier at all.

Then one day he came home in his new uniform and I hardly recognized him. Gone were the shirt, the suspenders, the gabardine trousers, and the broom handle. Instead, he carried a .303 rifle with a shiny dark-blue barrel and burnished brown gunstock, and looked dashing in khaki jacket and pants and big shiny black boots, a Glengarry perched jauntily on his head. Transformed, he looked every inch a soldier.

As early as I can remember, Dad had lectured me about manliness. Temperamentally, I was shy and timid and he must have considered this a major character flaw as he was always going on about what it means to be a "man." He would challenge me to put up my dukes, show me how to block punches by using my arms, how to jab. Boxing had been part of his rugged upbringing in Belfast and he wanted to pass on some of his boxing skills. After he enlisted, he constantly hectored me to keep my head erect, my shoulders straight.

"Soldiers don't slouch," he'd bark.

Dad was still training in Peterborough when Mom enrolled me in first grade at St. Peter's elementary school for boys. Mom bought me a new suit for the occasion: blue wool shorts and jacket, white shirt and a tie printed with bluebirds. Then she made me a small lunch. As we left the tenement for the short walk to the school, she planted a hat, more a beanie with a small peak than a real hat, on my head.

"Your dad wore hats like this when he went to school," she told me.

Approaching the school on Reid Street, a monstrous three-storey, red-brick edifice surrounded by a black iron fence, I noticed other boys being escorted by their mothers all wearing gloomy faces. Mom must have seen the vinegar expression on my face for she kept reassuring me: "Your dad loved school, Jim."

After entrusting me to Sister Angelica, the smiling grade one teacher, Mom waved goodbye and left, but not before admonishing me to behave. Like all nuns in those days, Sister wore a black wool habit and a black veil, with a high starched white band across the forehead, and had big black beads that hung from her waist and clicked when she moved.

"Be brave like your father," she said. "And don't forget to eat your lunch."

I met Dink Potts (he went by the moniker D.D. around the school) for the first time in the schoolyard at recess. Surrounded by his two pals, second graders like himself, he stepped in front of me and shoved me to the ground, knocking my beanie off. When I tried to get up he pushed me again, this time harder, and I scraped my knees raw on the concrete walkway.

"Look at namby-pamby," he glowered, tossing my beanie in the air. Gangly and well built, D.D. had a brush cut of thick coppery hair, large bony fists, and a brazen expression, and I quickly learned all about his reputation as a bully. Though Dad had taught me to box, I was paralyzed, too scared to fight back. Just as he was about to charge me again, Sister Luke, the principal, rang the bell and we assembled in the school basement for the march upstairs back to the classrooms, but not before D.D. got off one last shot.

"I'm not finished with you yet, shit-face," he snarled, smirking.

True to his word, D.D. made my life miserable. I became the target of his taunts, his punches, his shoves. He even made up a little jingle: "Clarke, Clarke, let a fart, blew the engine all apart." Often, he'd sneak up behind me in the schoolyard when the nuns weren't looking and swat the back of my head. Or he would grab my sweater and yank me toward him till my face almost touched his pug nose.

"Frog," he'd sneer, sounding like Edward G. Robinson in the gangster movies, and then he would shove me backward onto the ground, flat on my back.

One game I excelled at was marbles and I'd amassed a large collection of gorgeous glass globes of every variety: solid coloureds, apple cores, and even a few of the most coveted of all – big old-fashioned bonkers almost the size of golf balls. I stored my prized collection in a large tomato can in the summer kitchen.

One afternoon I was taking aim at a beautiful red apple core when I felt a sharp blow between the shoulder blades. The jolt pitched me forward onto the ground, grating my chin and spilling my bag of alleys. When I glanced up I saw the coppery glint of D.D.'s hair.

"Your dad's no hero!" he sneered. "He's a coward!" and his friends who'd encircled us howled with laughter.

"You're a jerk, Potts!" I yelled.

To this day I don't know what emboldened me to say it, maybe it was the slur on Dad's bravery, but the words just hopped off my tongue. D.D. grabbed my hair and shoved my head to the ground, grinding my face in the dirt.

"Shit-face needs his mouth scrubbed out," he said just as someone shouted "Bitties!" and he released me. Feet pattered in all directions. I looked up and glimpsed the pale faces of the nuns in the Black Maria, as we dubbed their bus, heading back toward the Mount.

One day, not long before Christmas, D.D. called me a pea-souper and gave me a split lip. When Mom got home I told her everything.

"No one likes a sissy," said Mom. "The next time he attacks you, hit back, you understand, that's the only way to stop a bully."

Gabby, who like Mom was prickly proud of her French ancestry, and took particular umbrage at racial insults, weighed in: "Don't let the *maudits anglais* push you around, Jeem," she said, her fierce brown eyes lighting up. "Remember, you got proud French-Canadian blood in your veins."

Mom had been raised as a tomboy on a farm with six brothers and she knew how to use her fists. She had been suspended briefly at work for giving the head waitress, an Englishwoman who'd called her a "frog," a black eye. No one cast aspersions on her ancestry and got away with it.

A couple of days later, I was walking home with a school chum, Pete Riley, when D.D. and his gang cornered me on the walkway beside the Cathedral. D.D. again called me a "frog" and punched me on the shoulder. Maybe Dad's lessons had finally sunk in, for when he stepped forward to swing again I jabbed him square on the face and bloodied his nose. The sight of his own blood shocked, then enraged him. But when he lunged at me I stiffed him on the jaw with another hard jab. The jab rocked him, buckled his knees, and sent him sprawling to the ground. That was the turning point. He got up slowly, brushed himself off and said, "Okay, shit-face, you win, this time," then shambled away, dabbing his shirt sleeve against his bleeding nose.

On the way home, Pete couldn't restrain his joy. "You showed him, Jimbo, you showed him!" he said over and over.

Mom and Dad told me that they were proud I had stood up for myself, and that evening Gabby rewarded me with an extra piece of fudge. "We're all proud of you," she said, "you taught that *maudit anglais* a good lesson."

Mom wanted to make Dad's last Christmas special and she bought some new silvery glass pine cones and grape-cluster ornaments for the Christmas tree. Two years earlier, I'd created quite a stir in Kresge's when, with my heart set on a red metal fire truck with a moveable ladder and a steering wheel that turned, I had sprinted up and down the aisles of the store, Mom chasing me, customers gape-mouthed, as I hollered at the top of my lungs, "I want a fuck! I want a fuck!"

All of us helped decorate the small spruce tree that Mom had bought at the market. Mom crowned the tree with her favourite ornament, a made-in-Germany Santa Klaus that she had bought before the war.

Christmas morning I was overjoyed to discover the Kresge fire truck that I'd been so crazy about under the tree. Unbeknownst to Mom, Dad had invited Young Irish and a couple of his buddies from the training camp over to the house and by early afternoon they were all well into the booze. You could tell from Mom's cross expression that she was miffed by their presence; she had her heart set on a private family celebration.

Young Irish was a natty dresser who wore well-tailored suits, black gleaming shoes and a homburg hat. He would often stand next to the grassy boulevard across the street and crook his baby finger to summon me and my sisters. As we watched bug-eyed, he would reach into the grass and his puffy blue lips would pronounce "Abracadabra!" and "Presto!" and nickels, dimes, and quarters would flash between his diamonded fingers. Mom always warned us never to take his money, that he was a gambler who drank too much just like his father and didn't pay his debts.

As the party unwound and the drinking continued unabated, Dad turned maudlin and took down his mother's picture from the wall, pressing it against his chest, exalting her many virtues: what a courageous woman she was, how she had raised seven children alone on the paltry salary of a doffing mistress in a Belfast linen factory, and on and on. Still seething at the uninvited cronies who were spoiling her Christmas, Mom called her his "old lady" and a "heartless bitch" for having sent Dad away at such a young age.

Dad was in the middle of a long tirade against Hitler when his eye caught the Santa Klaus atop the tree: "There'll be no German crap in my house!" Stumbling to the tree, he reached to take down the tree-topper but lost his balance and fell headlong into the small spruce, sending it and all the ornaments crashing down. The sound of splintering glass brought Mom rushing into the parlour to find all her beautiful decorations, including her precious Santa Klaus, shattered on the floor. She burst into tears and ran to her bedroom.

That evening, long after everyone had gone, I heard Mom in the kitchen chewing at Dad; how he'd ruined her Christmas, and inveighing against the war and his enlistment. Her railing went on for some time until Dad finally huffed out of the room, slammed the kitchen door be-hind him, leaving an eerie silence except for Mom's sobbing in his wake. As Mom had guessed, this proved to be our last Christmas together before Dad was shipped overseas.

His regiment marshalled in Central Park, grim and res-olute men in full battle dress, rifles at the slope, barrels shining in the sun, arms swinging in perfect unison, as they marched to the CPR station on George Street, where the waiting train hissed. Bagpipes blared as soldiers and loved ones hugged and kissed and wept. Dad was in a jaunty mood. When the second whistle blew for boarding he did a little jig on the platform, waved, and blew us all a last kiss before turning on his heels and, without a backward glance, disappeared into the waiting train, leaving us stranded on the platform, feeling like the first casualties of a war we didn't understand. As the soot-belching hulk of a train slowly chuffed out the station, I glimpsed Dad's grinning face smudged against the window of his coach. I wouldn't see him again for four years.

Part Two

THE WAR
THAT NEVER ENDED

STUPID WAR GAMES

The war became a ghostly presence: balls of string, lard for explosives, bundles of newspapers, tinfoil, old pots and pans, discarded clothing, propaganda movies, Pathé newsreels, Dad's grey-blue letters, ration coupons, Victory Bonds, 25-cent saving stamps (16 stamps for a four-dollar certificate which the government promised to redeem at the end of the war for seven and a half dollars), posters portraying unspeakable atrocities, games – Bomb Berlin, Blow up the Enemy, Victory Bombers – all were reminders of a terrible life-and-death struggle taking place across the ocean. Even Laura Secord chocolates packaged their sweets in cardboard tanks that had lift-off turrets.

This powerful, brutal enemy terrorized me. Every Saturday afternoon, newsreels at the New Centre Theatre showed U-boat survivors being plucked from the freezing Atlantic, the black specks of planes, more like bees than death-dealing machines, tracing arabesques in the sky over the peaceful English countryside. Sometimes we saw the twisted wreckage of a downed Stuka bomber, a swastika on its side, and we'd cheer when we were informed that the Luftwaffe was getting a pasting.

Occasionally we'd see old newsreels of Hitler, the evil one: Sam Browne belt, lock of hair over his forehead, little black moustache, haranguing a crowd of howling followers, his ravenous mouth opening and closing, opening and closing.

I built model airplanes out of balsa wood, Spitfires, Hurricanes, Messerschmitts, Stukas, and Mosquito bombers, with tiny propellers and canopies and all the proper markings stuck on, which I hung from my bedroom ceiling above the window so that I could watch them sway in the breeze.

We played soldiers. When we chose sides, I wanted to be a German, which must have something to do with Dad having told me the Germans were good soldiers. The Japs were different. Japs were not only alien, they were also thought to be sneaky and cruel. Nobody wanted to be a Jap.

We charged up snow banks, letting out loud war whoops, crouched behind hedges and fences and lobbed snowball grenades at each other. We wore wool-lined leather helmets with earflaps like the pilots in the movies and, with our arms extended as wings, school bags strapped on our backs for parachutes, we morphed into Spitfires and Messerschmitts and swooped down streets and through snowy yards, spitting out deadly bullets and tracers in terrible dogfights, gleeful as our foe crashed in flames into a fluffy snow bank.

I had a hidden camera in my head. Before dozing off at night in my chilly bedroom at the back of the tenement, I became the hero of daring war exploits, adventures that ran on night after night like the *Hopalong Cassidy* serials at the

Regent and, without missing a beat, I learned to tune into my fantasy exactly where I'd left off the night before, let it unfold like a magic carpet. Bullets couldn't stop me; I was, like my father overseas, invincible. He was my hero. I would invent stories, trumpeting his feats to my schoolmates whose fathers were not in uniform. I was smug, I was superior. Despite my fantasies, for a long time the grim reality of war and death seemed remote, unreal. But that soon changed.

In 1942 or 1943 the city held a mock blackout one night and everyone was ordered to switch off their lights and darken their windows. A siren pierced the night as streetlights were extinguished and Mom and Gabby scurried around to pull blinds and draw curtains. I peeked between the blinds in my bedroom and saw the powerful beams of two searchlights sweeping the pitch-black sky, highlighting the underside of clouds. Gabby glimpsed a military car as it slowly patrolled down our street, headlights dimmed. "Stupid war games, that's all," she muttered. A dread hung over the city and my imagination ran wild with images of saboteurs prowling about doing Hitler's evil work, blowing up factories, assassinating people in their homes. Scared to death, I had trouble falling asleep. That evening Mom brought a warm glass of milk to my bedside. "Gabby's right, Jim," she said, brushing her hand across my brow, "there's nothing to be afraid of."

Then, the real drama of war came home to me. I was playing war games in the York Trading yard with my friend Pete Riley.

"Hurry, planes comin'!" he yelled, pointing to the sky over Pinkus's scrap yard, "Nine-o-clock!"

Pete was standing on the steel platform at the top of the steel staircase at the rear of the York Trading building, right hand arched over his eyes. I heard a faint thrumming in the air and scrambled up the staircase just in time to see five mustard-coloured planes on the horizon in single-line formation glimmering in the sun. The air began to pulse, the thrumming turned to a deafening roar as the planes grew bigger and bigger, flying so low they seemed to skim the tops of roofs. "Man the ack-acks!" Pete ordered. "Messerschmitts.109!"

As the giant yellow birds streaked over our heads and thunder drowned out the rat-at-at-tats of our ack-acks, I thought I spotted the insect-like form of one of the pilots, helmeted, goggled and waving, but I wasn't sure. It all happened so fast. In a second or two, the planes were little more than specks on the horizon and then they vanished altogether like a dream.

"Boy, wasn't that somethin'!" gasped Pete.

"Yah, yah," I responded, too excited to dwell on my annoyance with him over having taken command. For the first time I'd seen real warplanes.

A GENTLE PUSH INTO THE WATER

I was afraid of water. I have a black-and-white snapshot of Mom and me standing on a flat limestone shelf near the old concrete bridge in Jackson's Park where the creek was damned for a swimming hole. I'm the tow-headed boy in a droopy bathing suit. Mom's wearing a white blouse and a long tight skirt that makes her tummy stick out a little. She looks unhappy, the same disgruntled expression she wore whenever someone snapped her picture. I'm shading my eyes with my right hand, squinting at the camera, grinning, no doubt proud of myself because I'd convinced her that I knew how to swim, when all along I'd been touching the rocky bottom of the creek bed, pretending.

Mom enrolled me in the Pioneer Class at the Y a year or so later. The huge red-brick building stood at the corner of George and Murray Streets, across from Confederation Park, four of five blocks from our tenement. It boasted an old gym with a running track, a swimming pool, table tennis and billiard rooms and, somewhere in its warren of rooms, a bowling alley. Every Saturday morning I'd pack my gear and arrive at the front desk in the lobby where the clerk would recognize me, buzz open a door to let me downstairs to the pool.

The Y soon became a second home. It was at the Y where I learned to swim. At the beginning I faked it at the shallow end, just like I did with Mom at Jackson's Creek, until one morning the coach, Mr. Ripley, convinced by my make-believe performance, took me to the deep end and pronounced I was ready. "You know how to swim, Jim," he declared, nudging me to the edge of the pool, me too afraid to reveal my secret. Standing on the edge of the deep end, shaking in my skin, I was unable to move till he pushed me gently into the water. With nothing under me to hold me up, I began to flounder, swallow water. I had no choice but to sink or swim and began to thrash my arms and kick my feet, finding, to my amazement, that I stayed afloat. Heart pounding wildly and gagging, I finally made it to the side of the pool where Mr. Ripley was waiting, a big grin on his face: "Attaboy, Jim! You did it!" he enthused. I lost my fear of water and soon became such a good swimmer he asked me to join the swimming team.

The following year, Phil Dugan, our grade five teacher, took all our class on a recreational outing to Lily Lake, a large pond rather than a lake. As I was drying myself off on the shore, I heard someone shout: "Carm's drowning!" and saw a classmate, Carmen Marrocco, floundering in the water a few yards from shore, his arms flailing, gasping for air. Mr. Dugan and the rest of the class stood there like stones. I dove into the lake, swam to Carm, grabbed his arm and managed to pull him, despite his thrashing, to safety. Mr. Dugan and the class hailed me a hero.

A few weeks later, I received in the mail a Certificate of Bravery from the Dow Brewing Company with my name in fancy gold lettering and a citation that stated I had committed an "act of bravery in risking my own life to save a fellow classmate from drowning." I was both surprised (I had no idea Mr. Dugan had submitted my name) and secretly delighted for I had always considered myself more of a wimp, easily cowed, than a hero. Mom was delighted, too. She hung the certificate on my bedroom wall and wrote Dad. "You done good, Jeem," Gabby declared.

I got another surprise. An airmail letter addressed to Master James Clarke clattered through the mail slot. "I'm very proud of you, lad," Dad wrote.

A CHAIR OVER THE TRAPDOOR

Mom found it tough sledding during the war years. Silk was in very short supply and the fashion industry came up with a liquid leg makeup called Neat. Neating was tricky business. Mom and Gabby took great pains to make sure the brown makeup was rubbed on smoothly and that the imitation silk seam down the back of their legs didn't wobble. They were not always pleased with the results.

By 1942, sugar, tea, coffee, butter, meat and gasoline were rationed. Families were issued coupons to ensure that everyone would be treated fairly. Mom frequently dispatched me to the butcher's on Charlotte Street with a note and some blue tokens the size of a quarter to purchase meat. Some restaurants had signs on their tables that read: USE LESS SUGAR, STIR LIKE HELL, WE DON'T MIND THE NOISE.

Dad's army pay, combined with Mom's wages and tips as a waitress at the Empress, gave her enough for rent, groceries, a small wage for Gabby, and a few other essential expenses, but only barely. At the end of her shift I would watch her empty the tips from her purse: pennies, nickels, dimes and quarters would come tumbling out, which she would count on the kitchen table and stack in neat rows before stowing them in the mason jar, which she kept in the cedar-lined hope chest in the bedroom together with her good linen and illustrations of her dream home. When tips were particularly good she would smile: "I done good today." By the end of the week, all her earnings would be depleted. We lived hand-to-mouth.

Every November she would borrow money from the Superior Finance Company to buy a tree and Christmas gifts – dolls or little carriages for my sisters, a Meccano or chemistry set for me. One Christmas I got my first hard-cover book, *Robin Hood*, and a Charley McCarthy doll that had a string with a metal ring at the end that I could pull and make his jaw open and shut. The next Christmas it was *Toby Tyler*, the sad adventures of a boy who runs away with a circus, which I read at night under the covers using a flashlight, tears pouring down my cheeks.

Mom was scrupulous about paying debts, and in the New Year she would commission me to deliver little white envelopes containing her finance payments to the company's office on Charlotte Street. By April the loan would be repaid in full and the company would reward her with a card with a gold border with her name in fancy lettering, proof that she was a member in good standing of the Honour Club. A new card would appear on the piano in the parlour every year, just beneath the pierced feet of the risen Christ.

Gabby was a good cook, a meticulous, even obsessive housekeeper, who always made sure we were fed well, did our homework, and got to bed early and out to school on time. But what Mom did not know, and what we were forbidden to reveal under threat of punishment, was that she also had a violent, sadistic streak. Through all of her childhood, my youngest sister Marilyn (Babe) was obese and my friends (including Shirl and me, I'm ashamed to say) called her cruel and belittling names such as "Fatty Arbuckle," "Fats" or "Fatty." Babe also wet her bed till she was eight or nine years old. Whenever this occurred, Gabby would go into a kind of choked fury and punish her by putting her in the cellar — a dank, dark malodorous hole with an earthen floor lit by a single bare hanging bulb, which you accessed through a trap door in the summer kitchen. As Babe screamed and her sobs came out in rolling waves, Gabby would install herself on a chair over the trap door with Cherie on her lap and taunt her, saying: "Bad girl, bad girl, the rats will eat you!" Only when Babe promised never to wet her bed again would Gabby let her out.

One time, when Babe's screams got to me, I tried to intervene and, in reprisal, Gabby lashed me across my bare legs with the maple switch she always kept handy, warning me that if I didn't mind my own business I'd get the same treatment. The tenement was booby-trapped with tension. Only in hindsight did I grasp the trauma Gabby's self-dramatizing and manipulative ways caused.

Later that winter, Mom had saved up enough blue coupons to buy calf's liver for everyone, a rare and expensive treat at the time. Though we kept some beef liver in the ice box for the dog, Gabby insisted that Cherie get her fair share, and, when Mom got back from work and found out that Cherie had been served some of the calf's liver she flew into a rage.

"The calf's liver was for the children, not the dog!" she shouted. But Gabby was unrepentant, insisted that Cherie deserved the best. "My dog is my baby." The argument seemed to be getting nowhere when Gabby's mouth suddenly twitched, her head rocked back and she shot up from the kitchen table and kicked Cherie in the belly, sending her flying halfway across the kitchen, yowling and scurrying for cover under the stove. We gasped in shock as Gabby then fled out the back door in her thin cotton housecoat and hurled herself into a snow bank in the backyard, where she sat blue and shivering, teeth chattering, for the longest while, spurning our entreaties to come in. Mom never bought calf's liver again. Sometimes at night I can hear Babe's screams.

LIFT HARDER
FOR THOSE WHO CAN'T

Every opportunity I got I would escape the tenement. I would run to the fire hall. I loved to spend evenings with Hank Hanson, a bodybuilder who kept weights and barbells in the basement of the hall. He liked to pump iron. In the 1940s, friendships between men and boys seemed natural and were not filtered through the social screen of suspicion and anxiety about potential abuse. I would watch, rapt, as he went through his barbell and dumbbell exercises, presses, squats and dead lifts, his skin glistening with sweat, amazed at the size of the rippling muscles in his legs and torso. I also admired his belt with its metal image of Charles Atlas, the other muscleman I worshipped, on the buckle, hefting the globe on his back. Hank showed me how to use the equipment and had a couple of sayings he'd repeat when I got discouraged about my progress: "Pain is only weakness leaving the body," and "Persistence is the key to all training." In time, he became a mentor and hero just like my Dad overseas.

For years at Christmas, Hank and the rest of the firemen collected castaway and broken toys, raised funds throughout the city for paint and supplies. And I'd beaver away for hours with Hank and the other men in the basement of the hall every fall, fixing and painting bikes, doll carriages, dolls, wagons, carts, scooters, metal hook and ladder trucks, sparking pop guns, train sets, and jack-in-the boxes. Sometimes I would accompany Hank and others in the truck on Christmas Eve as they made their rounds, distributing gifts to needy families all over the city.

It took two trucks running continuously for 18 hours to distribute repaired toys to hundreds of children, many of them with absentee fathers like mine. Lugging the boxes was tiring, and when I'd start to flag Hank would give me a pep talk. "Be charitable, Jim," he'd say. "Lift harder for those who can't."

I'd also help the men clean and dust the trucks and fittings, polish the floors, sometimes go out with the electrician, Vic Rome, to check the 42 or so alarm boxes on hydro poles, at hospitals and public buildings scattered throughout Peterborough where we'd install new batteries and repair broken parts. Hank Hanson showed me the fireman's rescue hold, and carried me up a ladder to a flat roof at the back of the fire hall. Being suspended in mid-air, high up the ladder and gazing at the men down below, was scary but not as scary as the trampoline. The trampoline was a round tarp with springs on an iron ring around the outside used in rescue operations. Once, when I was watching some of the men jump off the flat roof at the back of the hall into the trampoline, Vic asked if I'd like to try.

"Sure, it looks like fun," I said. But when I got onto the roof and looked down, I got butterflies in my stomach and my legs started to shake. Despite the chorus of encouragement from the men down below, "You can do it, Jim!" I lost all my bravado. I heard Vic's voice above the chorus: "Be brave like your dad." Firemen and soldiers are supposed to be courageous, I knew, and I wanted to be just like them, but I was too petrified, couldn't muster enough nerve to jump and I finally had to climb down, defeated and teary-eyed. I felt ashamed, convinced that I had let Dad down.

When my sisters, who had witnessed my terror from the York Trading yard and reported to Gabby what had happened, she was furious, called me a *fou* for attempting such a dangerous jump. And she then blasted the *maudit* firemen for endangering my life. I got no dessert that evening and was sent to bed early. The episode also provided her with more ammunition in her ongoing battle to keep me from the hall.

"He'll get himself killed, Flo," I heard her say when Mom got home.

A few weeks later, when I told my friend Hank about the incident (he was on the other shift at the time) and how badly I felt not jumping, he pooh-poohed the whole episode.

"Hey, Jimmy, lighten up," he said. "Take it from me, kid, it's no disgrace."

"But that's how I feel."

"Let me tell you a secret, pal," he went on. "You're not alone, I'm afraid to jump myself."

"Is that true, Hank?"

"Honest to God, cross my heart," he said, drawing a hand across his chest. "And I know several others, including Vic, who refused to jump."

Hank's words buoyed my spirits.

AN INTOXICATING
FEELING OF POWER

Before I was introduced to Pete Riley's parents, I'd watched them in church at the 10 o'clock Mass on Sunday, seated in the front pew, fingering their rosaries in silent prayer. Compared to the slack religious practices of my home, they impressed me as exemplary pious Catholics, the kind the nuns were always extolling at school, and I felt a little intimidated. I noticed that every time Pete acted up or didn't pay attention during Mass, Alice, his mom, would quickly lean across the pew and scold him.

The first time I met Pete Riley's mom in their home she scrutinized me up and down, gave me a tight smile and asked where I lived.

"Behind the fire hall," I told her. She arched her thin blonde eyebrows and the tight smile vanished.

"Oh, I see. And what does your daddy do, Jim?"

"He was a bellhop at the Empress."

"Oh, I see."

"But now he's a corporal in the army," I went on, to which she didn't reply, but eyed me suspiciously.

"And your mom, Jim?" she asked, after a pause.

"She's a waitress at the Empress."

"Oh, I see," she said again. "And who looks after you and your sisters when she's working?"

"We have a housekeeper, Gabby, from Quebec."

Alice was a stay-at-home mom with blonde curly hair, a puckered, pouty face, and beautifully trimmed fingernails that she painted bright red. Pete's father, Ollie, a trim, finicky man with a pencil moustache and a slight stammer, was the assistant manager of the local Dominion Bank. They lived in a large brick house with a wraparound veranda not far from the school. Pete was their only child.

After that first conversation, Alice became less cordial, and though I often visited Pete's home to play and help him with math, I was never invited to dinner or to stay overnight. The few times Alice spoke to me her frosty formality unnerved me. Mom told me not to be concerned: "She's a bluenose who thinks she's better than everybody else, son, that's all." Gabby wasn't so generous. She called Alice an "English beeech" and warned, "You ought to stop helping her stupeed boy with his homework."

Pete and I hung around together and he'd often drop into the tenement for cookies or a sandwich after school. Tall, skinny and bespectacled, he had an angelic studious face that belied his character. In truth, he was full of devilment and daring. We used to snitch apples and oranges from the bins at Basciano's, a small fruit store on Park Street not far from Pete's place, and it's a tribute to our skill or, more likely, our good luck that we were never caught. Our petty thievery soon branched out to Millards, a sports shop nearby where peashooters and yo-yos beckoned us. While I was a willing accomplice in these escapades, Pete, despite his prim Catholic background, was usually the instigator.

One evening after Pete left our tenement, Mom drew me aside in the parlour and told me in a hushed voice that Alice and Ollie were not Pete's "real" mom and dad, that he was adopted.

"Adopted?" I blurted. I had no idea what "adopted" meant. The word, which had never crossed my mind, made my head spin, as though Mom had just handed me forbidden fruit.

"I mean, Pete was someone else's boy," Mom explained, "and went to live with them as a baby."

"But why?"

"Why's not important, son. His real mother gave him away as a baby to be adopted, that's all. What is important is that Pete doesn't know and must never find out."

Mom spoke as though she was imparting some deep dark secret; her conspiratorial tone made adoption sound sinister, especially when she went on to assure me not to worry, that I really belonged to her and Dad. "You're our natural child, not adopted," she said, smiling.

"But you must never, never tell anyone, promise?"

"I promise."

The year after Dad went overseas, Mom bought me a wagon at Eaton's. It had varnished red wood with royal-blue trim, red wheels and a handle. With my left knee on a cushion in the wagon, I would pump hard with my right leg, imagining I was a fire truck careening along the sidewalks at breakneck speeds to snuff out dozens of raging fires that were consuming buildings, fences and trees. I even carried a big tomato can filled with water for such emergencies. To stop the wagon, all I had to do was press my running shoe on the back tire and it would screech to a stop. I remember Gabby once whining to Mom: "He's wearing grooves in the soles of his good running shoes, Flo."

One day, I noticed a piece of steel in the shed of the Nelson Lumber and Coal Company next door. It looked like a horse's head with a shiny flat top that felt cool when you glided your hand along it. I told myself it had to be a piece of junk and enlisted Pete to help me boost it onto my wagon. Pete told me it was an anvil, used for hammering and shaping metal. We managed to hoist it onto the wagon and cart it across the CNR tracks to Albert's junkyard on Bethune Street.

"Watcha got there for sale, young fellas?" Albert, a stocky man wearing greasy gloves, asked, removing a glove and inspecting the anvil closely. "How much ya want?" he asked after a pause.

"Dunno. It's junk, I found it," I said. Albert looked bemused.

"Ya found it, did ya? Will this do you, then, young fellas?" he asked, plunking two quarters into each of our outstretched palms. Pete and I couldn't believe our luck. We grabbed the coins and raced out of the yard.

That Saturday, Pete and I went to the Centre Theatre on the north side of George Street. The format never varied: a newsreel, followed by a serial, usually a horse opera (the serial always ended at a critical moment where the hero is being chased by Indians and about to jump off a cliff, a hook to lure you back the next week), a cartoon, and then a full-length movie. The feature, I vaguely recall, was a Bud Abbott and Lou Costello comedy. Not only did Pete and I stay for all of the movies, but we splurged on pop and chocolate bars. We got home late.

The next evening I heard the front door bell ring. Mom and I answered it together. Ollie and Alice were standing in the doorway, side by side, sober-faced and rigid, their green Ford parked at the curb in front of the yellow hydrant. Mr. Riley recounted what had happened.

"I don't know how you're raising your son, Mrs. Clarke," Alice huffed, "but this is not how we're raising Peter. Mr. Riley and I have decided your boy's not a good influence on Peter, Mrs. Clarke. Nothing personal, of course, but we'd prefer the boys no longer associate. Your boy may be going nowhere, but we have plans for Peter, you understand."

I could feel the blood rushing to my cheeks. I had the strongest urge to run, but my feet wouldn't budge.

Mom looked stunned, her face ashen. After the Rileys left, Mom made me confess. By the time I finished she was crying.

"Get to bed. I've never been so humiliated in all my life."

Next morning she dragged me along the sidewalk to Mr. Nelson's office. Mom poked my ribs, made me doff my cap. Mr. Nelson, a stout, poker-faced man with a bald head, gave me a withering look, but said nothing. He tapped a yellow pencil on the wooden counter. Unable to take my eyes off the creases in his big earlobes, sagging leathery jowls, and red porous nose, I stood there in a trance, weightless as the hollow bones of birds.

Then, Mr. Nelson, wattles shaking, lips quivering, rattled on about my hero father overseas, "fighting Hitler for the likes of you," how betrayed he'd feel to learn that his only son was just a "low-grade thief." A low-grade thief! I felt trapped in pure shame, transparent to all as a petty thief.

I went home that day dragging an iron sled of guilt, wondering if Mom would ever love me again. I wanted to shout: "Never again, I promise. Never again!"

OF FEDORAS AND FUDGE

In grade 5 or 6, I received the highest mark in my class in math, 98%. I couldn't wait to tell Gabby.

After supper, I showed her the test result. Gabby held the paper at arm's length; her long fingernails gleamed red.

"Not so bad, Master Clarke," she said. "Adrian always gets 100% in math. Nicole says the teachers call him their 'little Einstein.'"

Gabby always compared me to her nephew Adrian, in Sherbrooke, the only son of her younger sister Nicole. I sweated over my books, determined to surpass my rival. I never succeeded. But how could I? He was a genius.

Then, one day Gabby showed me a photo of Adrian: a gawky kid in a brown suit, standing at attention in front of a brown brick wall, a brown fedora on his head. How stupid he looked. Only grown men wore fedoras.

Later, I spoke to Mom. "The way Gabby talks, he's almost perfect."

"No one's perfect, Jim. Don't you forget it," she replied. "Besides, he doesn't have a soldier father like you."

Gabby was a capricious despot. Sometimes on drowsy summer evenings she'd let us stay up till Mom rounded the corner of the fire hall after work, holding three cones of dripping ice cream, her sensible, low-heeled shoes clacking on the orange bricks. We'd run full tilt to meet her and she'd give us each a cone. What hosannas! Nothing could quench our boundless joy.

One evening, Gabby ordered us to wash up. She inspected our open hands. Dirty fingernails disgusted her. (She oiled her own hands every day with Jergen's lotion, and painted her long nails bright red, too). She peered into our ears and poked into our mouths. Failure to pass inspection meant no fudge. The fragrance of fudge filled our kitchen. I could taste the creamy substance on my tongue. Gabby would sit at the end near the stove, her dog, Cherie, across her lap, as snow rattled the windowpanes, the kitchen warm and cozy. Wearing a pink kimono and white furry slippers, she read the latest *Captain Marvel* comic book, and dipped her hand into a pan of fudge and slipped a square into her mouth, but not before she gave a morsel to Cherie. My sisters and I watched in silence as Cherie nibbled the fudge, licked her lips with her small pink tongue.

Gabby loosened her kimono, leaned forward in her chair, the signal for me to straddle behind. She loved to have her back rubbed or, sometimes, her hair combed while she read. I dug my hands between her shoulder blades, careful not to touch the straps of her brassiere. Her body felt warm against my legs. As I pushed my hands up and down her knobby spine, the skin rippled ahead of my palms, soft and oily. Gabby moaned and sighed. Sometimes, when I touched an itchy spot, she'd tell me to use my fingernails. My body felt strange. At 7:45, Gabby looked up from her comic. "Okay, enough," she said, and placed two small squares in my palm, while Cherie and my sisters each got one. "If you're good, you can stay up till 8:15 tonight." A few minutes later, she slid the *Captain Marvel* book across the oilcloth, told my sisters they could read it after me. Immersed in the adventures of the Captain and Billy Batson, I read as fast as I could, anxious to finish before the deadline. "Time for bed!" Gabby snapped, startling me. I was only halfway through and Billy was in a tight corner. I pushed our luck and asked for extra time. "Your time's up, brush your teeth," she said. "Why do you take advantage of my goodwill? Don't I look after you?"

It was true. Gabby kept the house spotless, she made us do our homework, she fed us. Why, then, was I so afraid?

A HOLE IN THE BOTTOM
OF THE HAT

Gabby, having been home for a week with her family in Quebec, had come back to us.

"Gabby's brought you a present," Mom said.

Gabby set a large cardboard box on the kitchen table, spreading both her hands over the box like a magician.

"What do you think it is?" she asked. "Want to guess?"

I shook my head.

"You're too excited, I understand," she said, beaming. While Mom, my sisters and I gathered round the table, Gabby ceremoniously lifted the lid off the box, reached in and pulled out a soft brown fedora. The fedora had a shiny black band with a wispy red feather on the side and a wide brim that turned down at the front. It smelled of must. "Adrian got a new one for his birthday," Gabby explained. "Adrian's got such a big heart, he said he didn't need two. We'll give my old one to Jeem. Wasn't that nice of Adrian?"

Gabby set the fedora on my head, adjusted the brim and tucked in a lock of my hair. "All the young boys in Quebec are wearing them nowadays." The hat was ugly. "And a perfect fit, too. Your dad would be proud of you." Then the dreaded words: "You'll be the envy of all the other boys at school, just wait and see."

Next morning, I mustered enough courage to tell Gabby I didn't want to wear the fedora.

"But this is Adrian's gift to you."

"Everyone will laugh at me."

Gabby's face hardened.

"Boys in Ontario don't know how to dress," she said. "You want your daddy to proud of you, don't you, Jeem?"

She made me put on the fedora.

"Go on. Now you look just like Adrian."

By the time I turned the corner at Rubidge Street I was desperate. I noticed a window well by the side of a yellow brick house and buried the fedora in the well, camouflaging it under old newspapers and leaves and, in the afternoon after school, I dug it up and wore it home. Gabby was at the front door. "Now you see, Jeem," she said cheerfully, "none of your friends made fun of you, did they?"

"Nope."

"All that fuss for nothing."

One warm sunny day, I went to the hiding place after school only to discover the fedora missing. I scrabbled on my hands and knees, rummaging through the newspapers and leaves, but the fedora wasn't there. I heard a twig snap and D.D. and two of his buddies hopped out from behind some bushes.

"Looking for your fedora, shit-face?" D.D. asked. D.D. hadn't forgotten the bloody nose I'd given him. "Okay, shit-face, you can have your fancy fedora." He rammed his fist into the fedora; the crown exploded.

"Your hat needed a little fresh air, that's all," he sneered as he and his friends ran off.

At home, in a breathless rush of words, I told Gabby how D.D. and his buddies had ganged up on me. "Only frogs wear fedoras," they'd yelled.

"*Maudits* English *sauvages*," she muttered. I breathed more freely. The fedora became history, yet another example of mistreatment by the *anglais*. Gradually, she lost interest in the hat and the hateful D.D. She took up the Hawai-ian guitar.

The fedora with the hole in the crown languished in our summer kitchen's rag bin for months until one day I looked for it, and it had disappeared. All I found was one red feather.

ABOUT HORSES

Jack and Maggie were neighbours. Mom referred to Jack as Maggie's boarder. Gabby was blunter: "They're living together," making their life sound unsavoury.

Jack, a man in his late 40s, worked at the Peterborough Lock Company as a locksmith. Gangly, thin and slightly stooped, he had bushy black eyebrows joined above the bridge of his nose, a square grizzled chin, dark-brown deeply set eyes, and marvellous hands. Jack would spread a dozen or so delicate lock parts on his kitchen table and quickly assemble them. "See, Jimmy, nothin' to it."

I asked if I could try. "That's what I like, confidence," he said. No matter how often I tried to work his magic, the parts refused to do my bidding. When I'd finally give up, Jack would sweep the parts into a little cardboard box: "Tomorrow's another day, Jimmy."

In 1941, not long after Dad went overseas, Connell's corner store at Charlotte and Aylmer put on a promotion. The contest rules were simple: the boy in whose name customers bought the most merchandise before Christmas would win a brand new CCM boy's bike. The bike hung in red gleaming splendour above the front counter.

Jack organized a campaign on my behalf. Soon, neighbours on our street, the firemen, Mom's co-workers at the Empress, and Jack's buddies at the lock company began to sponsor me. Customers flooded Connell's, buying up merchandise in my name. Even Gabby began rooting for me. When Christmas Eve arrived, there was a knock at the front door and Jack stood there, a big grin on his face, holding the red bike in his long arms. "We did it, Jimmy," he announced. "You've won!"

Jack had been an artilleryman during the First World War and he'd seen action in the trenches. With his briar clamped between his false teeth, he would tell me about his regiment in France and the horses that hauled the big guns. "Magnificent creatures, they were," he'd mumble. Often the pipe would go out and he'd just sit there lost in reverie.

"We had to drag those guns in mud up to our stomachs," he said. "Poor animals, it was hell."

He kept a pair of brass horses, Moses and Elijah he called them, in a glass cabinet beside his armchair, each horse rearing high on its haunches. I loved to take them out of the cabinet and stroke their golden manes and bellies, feel the cool smoothness of the brass. He'd set them on a table so that their muzzles and hooves almost touched. As he told me stories about the horrors of war, Moses and Elijah ceased to be brass ornaments. I could feel their powerful muscles, hear them snorting and whinnying as they strained under the weight of heavy howitzers. One day I overheard Gabby grousing to Mom. "Why's the boy always next door at their place? Maggie and Jack are always

stuffing the child with cookies and ruining my suppers."
After a pause she added: "Besides, what can a boy like Jeem
have in common with an old souse like Jack?"

"Jack's a good man."

"But don't you see, Flo, he's spoiling the boy."

"Maybe Jim needs a little spoiling," Mom answered.
"He hasn't got a father."

Gabby was right. Maggie, who was short and energetic
and had a slight limp, spent most of her day cooking and
baking. Every day about noon my sisters and I would rap
on her small kitchen window and chorus: "Any cakes or
cookies today?" and Maggie's powdery, white face would
emerge from the dark interior. She'd raise the sash win-
dow and set a plate on the ledge. We'd grab the treats and
dash off to our secret eating place in the bushes at the far
end of the York Trading yard. We didn't want Gabby to see
us. Then one day, as I was bouncing an India rubber ball
against a brick wall in the fire lane, I heard something, a
groan like a low drawn-out keening. I ran to Maggie's win-
dow. She was pouring the contents of a flat amber bottle
into the kitchen sink. Jack, unshaven and shaking, looked
stricken.

"Please, Maggie, don't. Don't."

"I've told you a hundred times." Jack collapsed and
slumped into a chair, his long arms dangling between his
long legs. Maggie wrapped the empty bottle in newspaper
and stuffed it deep inside a garbage container.

Early one Sunday morning about a month after the
pouring episode, there was a loud knock on our front door.

It was Jack, eyes bloodshot, limbs shaking. "I need a pick-me-up, Flo."

Mom, who had a soft heart for anyone in distress, including those whose lives were tormented and bent by alcohol, let him in. Sitting him down at the kitchen table, she fetched a bottle of India Pale Ale. Tilting the bottle with both hands, Jack drained the ale in two or three big gulps. "Oh God, Flo, I needed that!" He asked for another bottle, which he downed. Colour returned to his cheeks, the glassiness in his eyes disappeared.

A week or so later I was playing in the backyard when I heard a faint voice. "Over here." I saw a slight movement between a gap in the fence boards, two small chestnut eyes staring back at me.

"Jimmy, keep this for me," Jack said. There was just enough room for the bottle to squeeze through.

"Our secret, Jimmy. Okay, pal?" he said winking, and then he vanished. I set the bottle on the lower rail of the fence and camouflaged it carefully with twigs and leaves.

For months, bottles shuttled back and forth through the gaps in the fence. In the spring, I dug a hole at the corner of the yard near the summer room window and hid the bottles in a small wooden box I'd found in Pinkus's scrap yard, spreading earth and grass over the lid.

I woke to a dazzlingly blue morning. Outside my bedroom window, buds were beginning to sprout in the branches of the maple, giving it a pale-green hazy sheen. I noticed Jack in brown slippers and rumpled grey pyjamas.

He signalled me to meet him. White and unshaven, he was shaking badly.

"I need a snort," he croaked.

I ran as fast as I could to the hiding place: the bottle and box were missing. I searched everywhere. There was nothing, save some fresh upturned earth and an empty hole.

"The bottle's gone! It's not there, Jack." I'll never forget the cry Jack let out, the blood-curdling moan soldiers in the movies made after they'd been mortally wounded. The moan became a whimper. He disappeared.

I lingered in the yard a long time, trying to figure out what happened. I'd never seen Jack in such pain and turmoil, and though I knew it wasn't my fault I couldn't help feeling responsible, that somehow I'd let him down and as a result he was now going to suffer. It never occurred to me that by hiding Jack's booze I might today be labelled an enabler or co-dependent. To me, I was just helping a friend in need.

Rather than return to my house I went out by the railway tracks to Jackson's Park, to the tarry smell of railway ties, the sun striking sparks off the rails. At the park, I waded barefoot on the flat stones in the creek, smooth and slippery underfoot, breathed in the tart fragrance of pine resin.

When I got back in early afternoon, Dr. O'Brien's green Ford coupe was parked in front of Jack and Maggie's. Doc O'Brien was one of the few general practitioners in the city who still made house calls and the presence of his car always spelt trouble. I glanced up at Jack's bedroom, clambered onto his back shed and crawled along the tin roof to his window. Jack was stretched out on his bed, his arms at his side, lips parted, breathing laboured, drawn and white like someone on the brink of death. Convinced he was dying and that I was at least partly to blame, I climbed down from the roof.

Gabby was standing by the stove in the kitchen, arms crossed, Jack's bottle beside her. "Where did you get this?"

I wanted to make up a story, but the words stuck in my throat.

"Don't play dumb with me, Master Clarke," Gabby said, digging her sharp fingernails into the nape of my neck.

That evening, with my Charlie McCarthy doll in bed beside me, I felt I'd betrayed my friend Jack, and, because of my betrayal, he would probably die. When Mom came to my bedroom after work that night, I buried my head beneath the covers.

"Your friend Jack was very sick today," she said. "He drank a bottle of shaving lotion."

I'd never heard of anyone drinking shaving lotion.

"Is Jack going to die?"

"No, dear, Jack's not going to die. At least not this time. But you mustn't hide his liquor any more. Jack's his own worst enemy."

I promised I would never again hide Jack's liquor. A couple of weeks later, I went back to Maggie's window and tapped on the glass. Maggie emerged out of the dark like a shadowy x-ray figure, bearing a wooden platter of oatmeal cookies and a glass of milk.

WHO SAYS LIFE'S FAIR ANYWAY?

My sisters led separate lives. They had their own friends and games, hopscotch, dolls, skipping and so on. In winter, the firemen piled snow from the fire hall yard into mountainous heaps along the wire fence where my friends and I would dig an elaborate white underworld, tunnels and rooms in which we lit candles, creating a male bastion from which girls were rigorously excluded. There was a small garage at the back of the hall we loved to climb onto and jump into the fleecy snow banks. One Christmas, I persuaded Babe to dive off the roof into a snow bank, head first, and watched her nearly drown, head and torso buried deep under snow, brown corduroy leggings kicking the air. Thanks to Hank Hanson, we were able to pull her out before she suffocated.

There was one activity my sisters and I shared: the priceless gift of celluloid. Every Saturday during the war Mom gave us an allowance of 25 cents each to spend at the movies, a tidy sum in those days. Not only did 25 cents pay for the movie, but there was usually enough change left for a chocolate bar or popcorn and pop. There were three theatres in town to select from: the Regent, the New Centre

Theatre and the Capital. The biggest hits of the year were generally featured at the Capital, on the east side of George Street just south of Charlotte. Ever since Mom had taken me to see *Snow White and the Seven Dwarfs*, the first Disney full-length animated cartoon in Technicolor, I was smitten.

The Saturday movies provided a full afternoon's entertainment, starting with a newsreel that kept us up to date on the war. I still recall the effect that the deep rumbling voice of Winston Churchill had on me. Gene Autry, *The Singing Cowboy* as he was billed, was a favourite. He could engage in marathon fist fights with several bad guys at the same time in which chairs were tossed around, tables broken and chandeliers came crashing down, and yet he always emerged victorious, his pristine white ten-gallon hat still on his head. The movie usually ended with Gene pecking the leading lady on the cheek and riding his famous horse, Champion, into the sunset, yodelling and singing. But romantic scenes disgusted me and any hint of smooching made me and my friends squirm and provoked boos.

But if I was hooked by movies, my eldest sister Shirl was spellbound and sashayed around the tenement with the disdainful haughtiness of a star. She thrived in a make-believe world, gauzy and romantic, inspired by the celluloid magic of Hollywood. She was especially fond of musicals, watched *The Al Jolson Story* four times and knew every song by heart. She wouldn't miss any production that starred Bette Davis or Joan Crawford. Every time she passed a mirror she'd pause to suck in her stomach like one of her glamorous heroines. She loved Bette Davis's imperious manner and would re-enact scenarios from her movies by drawing the rooms of imaginary mansions in the dirt with a stick.

To cap her life of luxury, she'd conscript Babe to play the chauffeur who'd drive her to the portal of the mansion in our old blue wheelbarrow. Babe also filled the role of maid. If the maid was insolent or spoke out of turn, Shirl would exclaim, "Fresh!" and slap her on the face.

Babe got smacked so hard and so often in Shirl's improvised dramas that her cheeks flamed scarlet. Babe decided playing maid to Shirl's diva was no fun and quit.

Every fall the New Centre Theatre held a talent contest open to anyone. The show was broadcast live on the local radio station and one year my sisters Shirl and Babe both entered. First prize for the most popular performer was $25, a princely sum in those years.

Babe was shy, but very musical and possessed a lovely voice. Shirl, on the other hand, sang like Dad, with an abundance of panache, but frequently off-key.

On the afternoon of the contest my friends and I hunkered in the back row of the theatre, ready to heckle and hoot. Del Crary, the MC, gave each contestant a spirited build-up in his plummy voice, and after their numbers he tried to whip up enthusiasm from the audience, mostly family and friends.

There must have been 12 or 15 contestants before Babe's turn arrived. With perfect pitch and sweetness she sang the love lyric, "Always":

I'll be lovin' you, always
with a love that's true, always.
When the things you've planned
Need a helping hand
I will understand, always....

During the performance my friends and I, who disdained anything soppy, squirmed and made faces. After she finished, Del turned to the audience, his voice ringing with superlatives, but he could only elicit a few scattered, lukewarm claps.

When Shirl was called, she flounced onstage from behind the curtain, wearing a big grin. Grabbing the mike, she shouted out: "You Call Everybody Darling." She belted out the lyrics in a jaunty voice:

You call everybody Darlin'
And everybody calls you Darlin' too
You don't mean what you're sayin'
It's just a game you're playin'
But you'll find everyone else can play the game
        as well as you.

If you call everybody Darlin'
Then love won't come a knockin' at your door
And as the years go by
You'll sit and wonder why
Nobody calls you Darlin' anymore.

The audience, under Del's prodding, joined in and began to clap. Shirl put lots of oomph into her rendition, blew the audience kisses, and her showmanship made a big hit. After she was finished the theatre went wild, some stood and clapped, others whistled and cheered. Shirl upstaged everyone and waltzed off with the big prize.

As we walked home together afterwards, a beaming and proud Shirl clutched the small envelope containing her prize money, boasting to everyone we met that she'd won. Babe was abnormally quiet, but when she got home and saw Mom and Gabby waiting in the front hall, she broke into tears.

"It's not fair," she cried. "I sang better than Shirl."

"You were wonderful," Mom said. "Your dad would be proud of both of you."

"But it's not fair, it's not fair."

"You sang beautifully, dear."

"I should have won."

Babe would not be mollified. She sobbed in the parlour for a long time and, after Mom left for work, was still teary-eyed at supper.

"Oh, for goodness sakes, Maryleeen, stop!" Gabby finally barked. "You're making me sick with your whining. Who says life's fair anyway? Just get over it."

A WARNING

Punctuality. Gabby would carry the kitchen Westclox around the house and no matter the true time, the Westclox was the official timepiece, the sole arbiter of lateness. Being late, even one minute, merited punishment. During our one hour of evening liberty, my sisters and I pestered passersby for the time. We'd rush home at the last minute to find Gabby waiting, maple switch in hand, and Cherie yapping at her feet.

"You're late." She'd wave the clock in our faces and begin to flail our bare legs with the switch. Sometimes, the door would be locked and she'd yelp: "Go to the back door!" We would find it locked, and so we'd shuttle back and forth till her lust for punishment was sated. At other times, if the whim was on her, she would tell us to look through the mail slot. She'd splash our faces with cold water.

One of her favourite pastimes was the "treadmill." She would sit on a chair at the foot of the staircase, Cherie on her lap, switch at her side, and force us to march up and down the thirteen steps till our bodies ached. "Keep going till I say stop!" If anyone faltered she would swipe the back of our shins. Only when we were breathless, our calves criss-crossed with red marks, would the punishment cease. Then she would whisk us off to bed before Mom got home with a warning not to tell anyone.

In the war years, horse-drawn wagons in summer and sleighs in winter brought wood, coal, bread, milk, and ice to the tenement. On hot summer days, the arrival of the ice wagon meant a cool treat. If the ice block was too large for our icebox, the iceman would use his ice pick to chip it down to size on the tailgate of the wagon. Then he'd heft it into the house, holding the block with steel tongs and shove it into the ice box, leaving a welter of ice chips and splinters on the tailgate for us. We would happily suck the ice.

The horses were well trained; the driver would walk ahead and make a "k-k" sound and the horse would move on to the next stop. If the driver thought there was any danger of the horse being frightened or spooked (runaway horses were not uncommon), he would toss his horse anchor – a large flat chunk of metal fastened to the wagon with a long piece of leather – onto the road and the horse would stay put.

One noon, my sisters and I were walking home from school at lunchtime. I remember the day, December 14th, my birthday – a sunny but bitterly cold day. Gabby had promised me a birthday cake and creamed salmon with peas on toast for supper. The snow crunched underfoot, the chains of passing motorists crackled on the icy roadway. The Wonder Bakery sleigh veered round the corner at Aylmer and Simcoe with Barclay the driver, who was notorious in the neighbourhood for his cruel temper, slapping the reins and whipping his old horse, Nugget, to a gallop.

"Faster, faster, ya lazy bastard!" he was yelling. The horse slipped sideways on his steel shoes on a patch of black ice and crashed hard onto the pavement. Nugget lay on the road, whinnying, the muscles on the plane of his flanks shuddering, his big orange eyes glassy with fright. Steam flared from his nostrils.

The sleigh had stayed upright. Barclay leapt from the cab, crouched over the horse, whip in hand and kept shouting: "God damn ya, Nugget, get up!" His small eyes bulged as he rained down blow after blow on the old horse's skinny haunches.

Shirl and I both screamed for him to stop, but he was a wild man. Shirl clapped her hands over her eyes and began to sob. I heard someone whisper, "That horse's leg is broken."

Two police officers arrived. One grabbed the leather whip from Barclay's fist while the other, the one with three stripes on his jacket, drew his revolver from its black leather holster, and, ordering the crowd that had gathered to fall back, he shot the horse in the head. The acrid smell of gunpowder scorched the air. Nugget lay on the icy pavement, twitching, a trickle of bright red blood pouring from his nose. One big blank orange eye was wide open. Gabby said that the *"maudit"* driver deserved to go to jail. "How can anyone be so cruel and get away with that?" she kept saying. "It is not just, it is just not right."

WE ARE ALL JOINED TOGETHER

During the war, the nuns told me how my heavenly Father looks after me and those who feel abandoned. Their operating manual was a pale-blue edition of *The Baltimore Catechism*. Organized in a simple question-and-answer format, it summed up everything we needed to know about God, the Catholic faith and the big riddles of life: Why did God make you? Why were you put on earth? What happens after you die? Every morning, new questions and answers were assigned for memorization. The next morning, we would be drilled. Our answers had to be letter-perfect, no paraphrases, no fudging, and definitely no excuses or we'd get a tongue-lashing, or worse, a painful rap on the knuckles with a ruler. In cases of repeated mistakes, we were hauled into the cloakroom to receive the leather strap. Father Leo Walsh, the parish priest, would drop by to test our progress and, though I possessed an exceptional memory and usually got good marks in Catechism, I remember getting strapped once by Sister St. Rose, my hands burning like the back of Christ.

Everyone loved Father Leo Walsh. He had a broad smile, a mop of black curly hair, and always brought a big bag of candies to the school that he would dole out at the end of his visits. Father Leo was a big Maple Leaf hockey fan (a good hockey player, the rumour mill had it he'd even played Junior A for St. Mike's before the war) and we would often see him at the orphanage's outdoor rink, the ice the silvery sheen of new nickel, pink biting his cheeks. It was Father Leo who first told me about number 9, Maurice Richard, the scoring sensation of the Montreal Canadiens. "Keep your eyes on him," Father said. "He'll be a big star someday."

On Simcoe Street we didn't need to be converted. Everyone was a Canadiens fan. We followed the *Bleu, blanc et rouge* on the *Hockey Night in Canada* radio broadcasts. For all of us, especially Gabby and Mom, the brooding, volcanic, black-eyed "Rocket" Richard was a folk hero. He was the avenger of historic wrongs done to a conquered people. The hooking, slashing, and spearing by tough guys like Wild Bill Ezinicki of the Toronto Maple Leafs enraged us.

I had skipped a grade and was now in the same class as the tough guy, D.D. His coppery hair was now longer, but D.D.'s princely swagger hadn't changed. One May morning during Sister St. Rose's Catechism class, he stood behind her back in the doorway of the cloakroom and mooned everyone. Sister suddenly whirled around in time to glimpse his naked bum before he hiked up his pants. Stout and pugnacious, Sister St. Rose had grown up on a farm. She wasn't someone to trifle with.

"So you think that's clever, Potts?" she said as D.D. strutted back into the classroom, a smirk on his face. As he passed her desk Sister, rolling up her billowy black sleeve, said, "You'll apologize right now."

"Says who?" D.D. sneered, clearly enjoying himself.

"Says me," said Sister. Her right fist struck D.D. square on the jaw, sending him hurtling across her desk onto the floor. He lay there stunned, dabbing his bloody lip with the back of his wrist.

"Do you want more, Potts?" Sister asked, balling her small red fist again.

"Please, no more, Sister, please, no," D.D. whimpered. He started to sob.

"Go back to your seat."

I became an altar boy and learned by heart all the acolyte responses, including the *Confiteor* in Latin. One Sunday evening, waiting for the priest to arrive for Holy Hour, we were waiting in the vestry, garbed in our black soutanes and white surplices, when Pete Riley jokingly suggested I hear his confession. I slipped into the darkened confessional with its velvet curtains and sliding panel, donned the priest's stole that was hanging on a hook, and pretended to absolve Pete of his horrific sins. Everybody split their sides laughing until Father Leo showed up, observed what was happening and immediately reached behind the curtain and plucked me out of the booth like a fish out of water.

"I'm surprised, Jim, you of all people," he said, glowering at me. I hung my head in shame.

"We were only playin'..."

"Playing, you say?" he said, whipping the stole from my neck, his face florid. "Don't you know what you did was a sacrilege? And your father overseas, too, fighting for his country," Father continued, "what do you think he'd say?"

There was a long pause. "I'll overlook it this time, Jim," he said, cupping his huge hand on my shoulder. "But don't ever let it happen again."

I couldn't believe my luck.

"And one last thing, Jim," said Father. "Don't forget to go to confession."

"I will, I promise, Father. I will," I stammered. And I did.

In November 1942, at El Alamein, a battered British Eighth Army broke the German line, and by 1943 the German Afrika Korps had abandoned its Italian allies who were in full flight. In the summer of that year, Canadian soldiers joined Montgomery's Eighth Army for the invasion of Sicily and the hard struggle up the long, mountainous boot of Italy. By September, at Stalingrad on the Volga River, the Soviets had surrounded and decimated an entire German army, 22 divisions. The end of hostilities and Dad's return did not seem so far off.

1943 was also the year Mom's dad, who was dying of stomach cancer, came from Quebec to stay with us for a while. Pépère, as we called him, slept on a cot beneath the stairway in the hallway downstairs. Every day, tall, stooped and gentle, he'd ensconce himself in the armchair in the parlour, light his pipe and pore over the newspapers. He kept me abreast of the news.

"The tide is changing," he told me. "Soon the Allies will be opening a second front and your papa will be there."

"Will he be killed?" I asked.

"Don't think like that, Jim," he replied sternly. "Remember, your papa's in God's hands; all we can do is trust and pray. Do you pray for your papa, Jim?"

"Sometimes."

"Good, Jim. God answers prayers."

"Will I ever see him again?"

"Of course you will," he said. "Don't worry, he'll be coming home sooner than you think."

As Pépère talked, his pipe would go out. I'd hold a match over the bowl to help him relight. Mom told me he did not have long to live. At night, I'd hear him groan under the stairway, the slap of Mom's bare feet on the linoleum, and the clacking of the kitchen cupboards as she fetched his pills, her soft voice talking to him like a baby. I heard him say: "I want to die *dans mon pays*."

One morning before dawn, Mom shook me awake. "Pépère's sick." I raced the two blocks through the rain in my new white running shoes to Dr. O'Brien's home, pounding frantically on the door. "Quick, quick! Pépère's sick!"

Pépère returned to Quebec. Mom, teary-eyed, bundled him into the back seat of Mr. Howell's blue taxi, a '39 Ford, for the long trip home, wrapped in a blue blanket, his battered brown fedora on his head, sucking his pipe. After his death, for the first time (though I couldn't have put it this way at the time) I understood something about the brevity of existence, how each of us is struck to breathless stone and the absence of a loved one leaves a permanent wound. I eavesdropped on Mom and my Aunt Marie who were talking and sipping brandy in the kitchen, Mom mumbling over and over, "His time had come," as though words had power to heal, learning we are all joined together, how love can only be broken one link at a time.

A few weeks later, making sure that the old caretaker of the cathedral, Mr. Armstrong, did not see me, I snuck up to the top of the cathedral steeple. I climbed the splintery scaffolding, higher and higher into the narrowing cone. The wind roared, the steeple swayed. I came to the ball and cross and could go no farther. Through a crack in the metal sheeting I glimpsed my world below; our street, the tenement, the fire hall, all my familiar haunts, too small now, it seemed, to contain all the sadness I felt in my heart. Up there in my high perch I prayed that Dad would come home safe.

SOMETHING'S WRONG AT HOME

Once or twice a week, thin blue letters – "bluebirds," my sister and I called them – would tumble through the mail slot in the front door onto the floor, bluebirds ruffled from their long sea voyage. The censored letters, post-marked "Somewhere in England," had an aura of mystery. Most were for Mom. Sometimes there would be one or two addressed to my sisters and me. Mine were always addressed to: MASTER JAMES HENRY CLARKE, which I found odd.

One day I asked Gabby what "Master" meant.

"Just a stupeed English custom," she replied. Gabby disliked the English and had little enthusiasm for the war. "We're always fighting England's battles," she'd rant, sometimes adding that Dad should have stayed at home and taken care of us instead of chasing *"la gloire."*

After a while, the accumulated letters took on a life of their own. They flooded the old wooden summer kitchen floor like a pale blue sea. From time to time, Mom or Gabby, exasperated, would gather them up and stack them in Mom's hope chest.

My sisters and I loved to sneak into the summer kitchen and read the ones to Mom which always began "My dearest Darling" and were full of sentiment. Dad was always promising to mend his ways, give up the bottle, and be a better father and husband. Mom's life-long dream was to own her own house, and Dad's promise that once the war was over his "gratuity" would go toward a down payment on a new home rainbowed over all her hardships and disappointments. The letters always ended with "Till we meet again" and a flourish of xxx's and ooo's. The saccharine sentiments, so unlike the Dad we knew, made my sisters and me giggle.

The letters asked that Mom send cigarettes, tobacco, and chocolate. Mom and Gabby spent long evenings in the kitchen carefully packing brown cardboard boxes for shipment overseas, all the while nipping from a mickey of rye they kept on the floor by the side of the stove. As she rambled on about the end of the war and the new life we would all have in our new home, Mom would take on a wistful look.

"Imagine, all of us in one of those new homes with a lawn and garden," she'd say, eyes misting. "Won't it be great, Gabby?"

Gabby remained sceptical. "We'll have to wait and see, won't we, Flo," she'd say, adding, "A leopard doesn't change his spots."

I overheard them in a heated argument. "Why's he always asking for cigarettes, anyway?" Gabby asked. "He doesn't even smoke"

"They're having a tough time over there,"

"I'll bet, playing the big shot, if I know your Sammy."

"For God's sake, Gabby, shut up," Mom said and stalked out of the kitchen.

The letters buoyed Mom's spirit and after a few drinks she and Gabby would break into song – "Wish Me Luck as You Wave Me Goodbye," "Praise the Lord and Pass the Ammunition," "When the Lights Go on Again," and other wartime tunes. Sometimes, as Mom tucked me into bed, she would croon her favourite, "The White Cliffs of Dover," and when she came to the line "And Jimmy will go to sleep in his own little room again," she would stroke my brow as tears ran down her face.

In late October or early November, we noticed that Bobby Kelly, our freckle-faced classmate, was not himself. His face took on a mournful vacancy and he moped by himself by the iron fence at the back of the schoolyard, hands thrust deep in his pockets. "I think something's wrong at home," Pete said.

In early December (Bobby was absent that day), Sister Luke, the principal, made an unexpected visit to the classroom. Black hairs protruded from her long aquiline nose. She had a withering stare. A hush fell over the class. Pale lips barely moving, she announced, "Bobby's mother has gone home." She asked everyone to pray for "the repose of Mrs. Kelly's soul" and said that the whole class, no exceptions, would be paying a visit to the Duffus Funeral Home on Water Street the next afternoon for prayers.

That night, I dreamt of a long black snake, eyes green and glittery. I woke up in a sweat. All next day, snow fell, huge wet flakes falling from the gun-metal sky. At 4 p.m.,

Sister St. Rose, a heavy black shawl wrapped over her broad shoulders and wearing ankle-high black galoshes, led us downtown to the funeral parlour. Dressed in corduroy breeches, wool-lined pilot helmets, the front flaps pulled down over our foreheads, we waded down the snowy sidewalk, our calf-length jackboots leaving prints behind us. I had never seen a corpse. Entering the parlour, the sickly smell of cut flowers made me choke. I was afraid to look at Bobby, curly red hair newly cut, in his navy-blue gabardine suit, standing next to his stricken father. Sister St. Rose lined everyone up and, one by one, made us kneel on the prie-dieu before the casket and recite a Hail Mary.

I was so overwrought the Hail Mary stuck in my throat. I couldn't take my eyes off Bobby's mom in the shiny box. With her thick coiffed brown hair, rouged cheeks and long bony nose, pink glass rosary entwined in her clasped hands, she looked like she'd just fallen asleep. The way everyone averted their eyes and crept around the room made me think they were afraid.

At supper that evening, I asked Gabby what it was like to die. "Why do you ask such silly questions, Jeem?" she said. "No one knows until they die."

"Where do people go when they die?"

"Have you done your homework?"

"I just want to know. Dad's a soldier, he could die anytime, couldn't he? I just want to know, that's all."

Gabby shrugged, annoyed by my persistence.

"Do your homework now," she said, a snarl in her voice.

When Mom got home (Gabby let us stay up that evening), I asked her what Sister Luke meant when she said Bobby's mom had "gone home."

"Good people go to heaven when they die," she said. "That's where Bobby's mom is right now, home with God, so stop worrying, Jim. We just have to trust that God takes care of all of us."

"Could Dad die, too?"

"How can you ask such a question?" she said. "Get to bed, you've got school tomorrow."

In bed I listened to the snow gusting against the windowpane. I wondered why no one wanted to talk about "going home." I felt the weight of a terrible secret on my heart. Standing in the schoolyard the next day, I found myself trying to hold onto the big, soft swirls of snowflakes before they melted.

BUT DON'T SAY
I DIDN'T WARN YOU

The CNR parked empty boxcars on the siding beside the York Trading building on Bethune Street and often the doors were left open. My chums and I would clamber into those cavernous echo chambers, strip off all our clothes and run around naked, dancing and whooping like the drunken Apaches we'd seen in the movies. The heady rush of doing something risky and forbidden, perhaps even sinful, was irresistible.

One evening, when four or five of us were cavorting naked, a new face popped up in the opening.

"Can I play too?" The stranger, a lanky boy with thick black curly hair and curious small brown eyes, was staring at us.

"What are you doing here?"

"It looks like fun," said the stranger, glancing around the boxcar at our bare asses.

"Who are you anyway?" I said.

"I'm Josh."

"Josh who?"

"Josh Finkleman. I live across the road from the Fire Hall."

"Okay, come on in," I said. Josh immediately shed his clothes and joined in.

Josh was the son of the new rabbi, Abraham Finkleman, at Beth Israel Synagogue on Aylmer Street. They'd just moved from Toronto.

After that evening, he showed up regularly in the York Trading yard. He was bold and fearless, and we became fast friends. We also became avid and skilled boxcar watchers, stationing ourselves at the side of the tracks, trying to outdo each other in identifying the markings on the sides of the boxcars as they rumbled by. Because it was fraught with danger, one of our favourite pastimes was hitching a ride on the side ladders of the cars and hanging on for two or three blocks before jumping off. We placed pebbles on the rails and watched as they got ground to powder by the giant wheels. If a conductor spotted us near the tracks, he would shoot out a cloud of cindery, acrid steam in our direction to scare us. When I brought home a flattened penny and showed it to Gabby, she rapped me on the head with her sharp knuckles. "Didn't I tell you to stay away from the tracks?" she shrieked, her mouth twitching. "You could get killed!"

Several weeks later, when I asked if I could invite Josh to the house to play Parcheesi, she seemed peeved.

"Is there somethin' wrong, Gabby?"

"Why are hanging out with that Jew boy, Jeem?"

"What's a Jew boy?"

"Don't play games with me," she said. "I'm talking about Josh."

"What's wrong with Josh?"

"You've read your Catechism. The Jews killed Jesus."

"But Jesus was a Jew," I said.

"Yes, but not like them. He was a good Jew."

"Why did they kill Jesus anyway?" I asked.

"They hated him because he was Christian, okay?"

"But I like Josh. We get along."

"Okay," Gabby said, "but don't say I didn't warn you."

Mom told me not to pay attention to Gabby. Mom bought from the Jewish shops in town and Mrs. Pinkus frequently asked her to serve at their home when they were having a private party or religious celebration. "The Jews pay good and always treat me with respect," Mom said, adding, "Remember, Jim, people get a little *fou* and envious of others who work hard and make money." Mom would often slip into French when she spoke to us (my sisters and I understood French though we didn't get much of a chance to speak it), which used to irritate Dad who'd bark, "Speak white around here."

Josh attended Central Public School and was one year ahead of me. He was a voracious reader and possessed a wide vocabulary, using words I'd never heard before, which he'd explain if I asked. When it was a word he considered I should have known, he'd sometimes lose patience and add, "Where have you been living, Jimbo? Under a rock?" He also shared his baseball cards, and now and then I would visit his apartment at the back of the synagogue to look at his stamp collection. Once, he loaned me his copy of *Moby Dick*. I read it in bed by flashlight under the blanket with the help of a dictionary.

His mom, Goldie, a plump woman with long black hair and eyes dark as dates, had a warm welcoming smile. Every time I saw her she was wearing a floral apron, cooking or baking. She would treat Josh and me to a slice of her honey cake and once she served us latkes; I had never tasted spuds so delicious. The apartment was chockablock with books and records, which Josh would play on their old windup Marconi gramophone.

One time when we were in the apartment alone, Josh switched on the short-wave radio and a voice came shrieking over the airwaves. The voice was distorted, fading out and then getting louder again.

"Who's that?"

"The Fuhrer, you twit, who else?"

We listened for a few moments then Josh turned off the radio. "My parents don't like me listening to that maniac."

Rabbi Finkleman was grouchy and aloof. Short in stature, he wore a black suit and a fedora, and most of the time he seemed absorbed in thought and oblivious to my presence in the apartment. I noticed that he and Goldie sometimes spoke a strange dialect. Josh explained that it was Yiddish, a mixture of German and Hebrew and other eastern European languages.

One day while we were playing in the York Trading yard, Josh showed me a magazine, *Sunbathing and Health*, that had black-and-white photos of smiling naked women on a beach, their private parts air-brushed. I knew next to nothing about lovemaking till Josh explained how the penis enters the vagina to lay its sperm and fertilize the egg.

"What's a vagina?"

"Don't be such a schmuck, Jim," he said. "The pee-hole, get it?"

"Pee-hole? How does that happen?" I asked incredulously.

"The penis and vagina both stretch, you twit." Josh proceeded to illustrate his meaning and thrust his right index finger into a circle made by his left thumb and forefinger. My nascent sexuality took the form of filling a thick scribbler with hundreds of drawings showing men and women splayed beneath each other or arched above each other making love in different positions, which I kept carefully hidden in my closet. (After the war Dad stumbled upon the scribbler. "Is this the smut they teach ya in that dogan school of yours?" he bellowed, ripping the scribbler in shreds and burning it in the potbelly coal stove in the parlour.)

Josh, who was reading a book about Abe Lincoln and his trip down the Mississippi as a young man, came up with the bright idea of navigating Jackson's Creek, all the way through the city to Little Lake. "It'll be a great adventure," he said. We set about cobbling together a raft from scrap lumber and old logs.

On a Saturday morning in April (Josh skipped Hebrew classes that day), we launched our little vessel at Jackson's Park. We poled our way through rocks and shallow stretches, past derelict baby carriages, old bed frames, crates and other castaways in the creek bed till we came upon a fallen tree across the creek just north of Hunter Street that effectively barred our passage, marooning us in the middle of the turbulent creek. Someone saw our predicament, contacted the fire department and we had to be rescued.

"I'm disappointed that you of all people would try such a hare-brained escapade," Chief Fraser chided me. "You could have drowned."

The Rabbi punished his son by forbidding him to see me for a month.

After the one month, I ran into Josh outside Hin Lee's laundry. He told me his mom and dad were out for the afternoon and insisted on showing me the synagogue.

The entrance to the synagogue was a plain wooden door just inside the vestibule of an apartment building. Josh unlocked the door. We crossed the threshold into a gloomy square room with two small arched windows and a back door. He handed me a skullcap.

"What's this for?"

"It's a yarmulke, twit. You wear it on your head. Don't you Christians know anything?"

"Why?

"Jews cover their heads in a synagogue out of respect for the Creator."

A burnished brass candelabrum burned in front of velvet curtains on the east wall where the Torah scrolls were kept in a cabinet, arranged in a standing position. Hebrew inscriptions and lions and eagles adorned the wooden doors of the cabinet, but the rest of the room was stark. In the centre of the room was a raised podium (Josh called it the *bima*) where Rabbi Finkleman, who was also the cantor, read the scrolls and sang. It was part of the rabbi's job to keep the candelabrum always lit before the Ark, Josh explained.

He fetched one of the scrolls and brought it over to the podium. We heard footsteps in the hallway. Josh gasped: "It's my father, I can tell!" We just had time to grab the scroll and duck behind the curtains before we heard the knob on the back door turn. As we stood behind the curtain, I began to shake. I thought we were doomed till we heard Goldie's voice.

"Abe, can you come back here for a moment, please?" Rabbi Finkleman immediately retraced his steps back to their apartment. Josh and I whisked the scroll back into the cabinet and bolted out of the synagogue. I never stopped running till I reached the tenement. Gabby caught me, still panting and trembling.

"Stop. I told you never to run in the house." She stared at me. "You look like you've just seen a ghost. What's wrong?"

"Nothin' at all."

"Did you get my laundry?"

"I forgot," I finally blurted.

Gabby glowered at me as though I'd betrayed her. "You forgot?" she repeated slowly, "And what's that thing you're wearing, Master Clarke?"

I'd forgotten to remove the yarmulke.

"It's nothin'," I said. "Josh gave it to me".

"The Jew boy?"

I didn't answer.

"Didn't I warn you about Jews," Gabby snarled, and with one swift, deft motion, she snatched the yarmulke off my head, stomped over to the kitchen stove and tossed it into the flames.

"That'll teach you, Master Clarke," she said. "Now go to your room."

A KIDDLE-DEE-DYVY TOO, WOULDN'T YOU?

Sundays, after supper, we would gather in the parlour around the old Jackson Bell cathedral radio Mom and Dad had bought before the war. Shaped like a church, the radio had a round cloth grill with a wooden swan cut-out over the voice box. During storms it was subject to static attacks, and sometimes it would let out piercing squeals in the middle of a program, often when Jack Benny was cracking one of his wry jokes, or Edgar Bergen and his impertinent dummy, Charlie McCarthy, were bantering with Mortimer Snerd. If Gabby was feeling generous, she would let us listen to *The Green Hornet* and *The Shadow*, Lamont Cranston's baritone intoning, "Who knows what evil lurks in the hearts of men? The Shadow knows," followed by a prolonged sinister laugh that gave me goose flesh. Often I would lie in bed in the dark staring at the head of the stairs, too petrified to close my eyes or move.

Gabby would sometimes play records on her 78-rpm player and our little tenement would swing to the sound of the big bands, Harry James, Tommy Dorsey, and Glen Miller, or the voices of Bing Crosby, Doris Day, and Dinah

Shore. On Saturdays, we would sometimes dial into *The Hit Parade* to listen to the top 10 tunes of the week. One of Gabby's favourites, which she sang ad nauseam, was called "Mairzy Doats"

> *Mairzy doats and dozy doats*
> *And little lambzy divey,*
> *A kiddley-divey too,*
> *Wouldn't you?*

A Hawaiian craze swept the country and Gabby spotted an ad in a magazine that promised she could learn to play the guitar "just like a Hawaiian" in only four easy lessons by using a unique method called the "Lettergram." Gabby wrote to an address in California, and a few weeks later the lessons arrived in a thick manila envelope. She had shopped around and had bought a second-hand Hawaiian steel guitar.

Gabby practiced for several months singing and playing one tune over and over.

> *The winds over the sea*
> *Sing sweetly aloha to me*
> *The waves as they fall in the sand*
> *Say aloha and bid me to land*
>
> *The myriad flowers in bloom*
> *Waft aloha in every perfume*
> *I read in each love lit eye*
> *Aloha, aloha, nui 'oe.*

Gabby announced that she was going to give a concert in the house after the Saturday movies and wondered if any of our friends might attend.

On that afternoon, three friends sat on the chesterfield with me, my sisters and others on the floor. Gabby sat in an armchair across from us, guitar on her lap, Cherie at her feet. Cherie started to yowl, jouncing up and down like she did when strangers rang the doorbell. Gabby took a deep breath. Cherie yowled so loudly she drowned out Gabby's voice. Doreen Booth, Shirl's skinny freckled-faced friend with flaming red hair, began to giggle, a giggle that spread until everyone in the room, except me and my sisters, was laughing. Gabby turned crimson, her mouth twitched. She rocked back. Letting out a yelp, she leapt to her feet, dropped the guitar and fled upstairs to her bedroom, Cherie at her heels.

For a long time we heard sobbing, and that evening she didn't come down for supper. When Mom got home, she went upstairs and comforted Gabby for a long time. That was to be Gabby's first and last concert. The Hawaiian fever soon passed. A year later, I found the guitar in a corner of the summer kitchen, gathering dust.

NIGHTMARES OF THE CARNAGE

During the war, the Y ran a week-long summer day camp for boys whose parents did not own a cottage and couldn't afford a regular summer camp. The activities included an educational component, such as bird watching at Jackson's Park. We also visited Canada Packers, the local slaughter-house, to learn how meat was processed. I was over-whelmed right away by the loud hum and grind of the huge machinery and the warm, sickening stench of entrails and blood. Bare-chested men in long aprons hooked the hind legs of squealing hogs to a chain and hoisted them upside down on a rotating conveyor track. Another bare-chested man stood on a platform, a long knife in his fist. As each pig swung past, he thrust the foot-long blade into its throat, sometimes as far as his wrist, to cut the jugular. Blood spurted from the wound. The hogs squealed and flailed on the track until they bled to death.

They took us into another smaller abattoir where we watched as a steer was prodded down a narrow walkway into a small pen. A man holding a big sledgehammer waited on an overhead platform. While ropes steadied the steer's head, the man took aim and swung the hammer down between the steer's eyes, shattering its cranium with a loud cracking thud. As the steer's legs buckled and it collapsed on the concrete floor, yellowy pulp poured from its nostrils and mouth. The blood and smashed brains nauseated me. I brought up all over my good shirt and felt my legs give way. Two of the guides had to help me out of the plant. I vomited again on the grassy boulevard. At home, I was sick in bed for two days. The carnage haunted me for several months.

When I told Josh about my experience, he told me his family ate only kosher meat slaughtered by rabbis. The animal is never stunned, he said, the ritual requires that it be conscious right to the end. Though I didn't tell Josh how I felt, I thought the practice was barbaric, and when I mentioned what he'd told me to Gabby she only shrugged, "Didn't I tell you to watch out? The Jews aren't like us."

As the war in Europe raged on, Mr. Dunford, the dogcatcher, waged his own canine war, patrolling the city on the lookout for strays. One afternoon that winter, Josh and I happened to be walking past his place, not far from the tenement, when we noticed his old Ford truck pull into his yard. There were several dogs jammed in the back. We crouched behind a neighbour's fence and watched him put on leather gloves and grab the dogs one by one, shoving them through a door in a big box he'd cobbled together from old crates. After they were packed in, barking and whining, he locked the door, rigged a hose from the truck to a hole in the side of the box, and started up the truck motor. He ran the motor a long time till the barking and whelping died away and silence fell over the yard. Then he unlocked the door, yanked the dogs out one at a time, and lined them up in a neat row on the snow. Flake by flake, snow dropped from the quiet sky as Josh and I watched their bodies turn to silvery fur.

Later that winter when I came home from school, Mom sat me down opposite her on the sofa.

"I've got bad news, Jim," she said. "Your friend at the fire hall, Hank Hanson, has had a terrible accident."

"What do you mean?"

"I'm sorry to have to tell you this, Jim, but Hank was killed in a fire at the old Woollen Mill this morning."

I blinked back tears.

"I'm sorry, Jim," she went on, "but bad things happen to good people all the time. Your dad would want you to be brave."

I rushed to my bedroom.

That night, I couldn't sleep for thinking of Hank. Next day, I ran all the way to the Woollen Mill at the foot of Charlotte Street. I sat down on the roadside curb, gazed at the old mill, a heap of rubble now speckled with fresh snow, stunned and mystified by the power of death. The top floors of the four-storey building had collapsed and huge bales of soggy, rotting raw wool that had dropped from the upper floors were still smouldering – the stench of the wool, akin to the smell of burnt flesh.

That evening, Gabby showed me the paper. The headline read: HERO DIES TRYING TO SAVE MATE. They said the fire was an inferno, that volunteers had found Hank's body and had identified him by his Charles Atlas belt buckle.

A GUTTER WOUND

The war never seemed to end. Then, in July 1944, a tall, pallid man wearing a clerical collar and a stocky military officer got out of a car and walked to our front door and rang the bell. Canon Robertson from St. John's Anglican Church put his arm around Mom's shoulder and led her into the parlour, followed by the officer and Gabby. Soon my sisters and I heard sobbing. After the two men left, we children rushed into the parlour to find Mom and Gabby seated on the chesterfield, holding hands.

"Your dad's been wounded," her voice like the whimper of a child.

"You mean he's dead."

"He's in a hospital in England, not killed."

"He'll get better, children, don't worry."

Next day there was a write-up in the Examiner together with a photo of Dad in uniform. CORPORAL CLARKE WOUNDED AT CAEN, read the caption, and the article went on to say that he had been shot by a sniper on the 8th of July, "a gutter wound" the medics described it, during Operation Charnwood, whose object was to capture the German stronghold of Caen. The article ended on a hopeful note, saying he was now in England convalescing and was expected to make a full recovery. Overnight, Dad became a local celebrity.

"The bullet went right through here," I said, touting his bravery to my classmates, pointing to my right temple and drawing an imaginary line through my ear. I felt more elated than sad; Dad was now a war hero.

Despite optimistic newspaper reports and Dad's cheerful letters, D-Day was not the end but only the beginning of the end. Headlines kept us abreast of the Allies' slow but relentless march across Europe. The Allies bridged the Rhine, the Russians swept across the Oder-Neisse, and the ugly black blot that had represented the Thousand-Year Reich on the maps in the Pathé newsreels shrank every day.

A jaunty light-heartedness began to lift everyone's spirits. The nuns caught this new feeling, smiled more often and told us repeatedly that peace was just down the road. Mom and Gabby talked of the happy days to come when Dad would get his gratuity and they would own a house, just like the one Mom had her heart set on. I saw them in the kitchen, eyes aglow, gazing at a newspaper ad: TAKE A PEEK INTO YOUR POSTWAR DREAM HOUSE, it said, and showed a sketch of a home that had air conditioning, wall-to-wall carpeting, a modern range and refrigerator. The ad encouraged everyone to buy Victory Bonds so that the dream could become a reality. Mom carefully cut out the ad and squirreled it away in her hope chest where she also stored Dad's letters. Gabby kept exhorting me to do my homework, to do as well at school as Adrian.

"You want your dad to be proud of you, don't you, Jeem?"

Maybe it was the English movies I had seen that featured John Gielgud, Lawrence Olivier, and Michael Wilding, with their dulcet and sophisticated accents, or maybe it was the simple desire, like Mom's, for a new beginning – but about this time, consciously or unwittingly, I acquired an English accent. I was transformed from a poor kid from the wrong side of the tracks into an urbane Englishman. British idioms like "crashing bore" and "bloody" crept into my vocabulary. Josh noticed the change and baited me. "You're talking like a schmuck," he snarled. "Got the flu, Jimbo, or something?" Pete Riley quipped. I was determined to reinvent myself.

When Sister St. Rose, who was teaching a public-speaking course, asked me to take part, I immediately responded: "Jolly good, Sister!" Each participant was expected to prepare and give an eight-minute talk. Sister knew that Dad had been wounded in the invasion of Normandy and she suggested that I could talk about D-Day.

"It's up to you, Jim," she said, "but it would give your talk a personal touch, wouldn't it?"

After hours poring over books, old newspapers and magazines in the public library I found enough material on Operation Overlord – the leaders, the roles of the Resistance, and the thousands of paratroopers who preceded the sea borne landing, as well as the five different beaches code-named Utah, Omaha, Gold, Juno, and Sword, where the Allies landed – to stitch together a credible speech to support my thesis that it was Hitler's failure to stop the Allies in Normandy that permitted them to push inland, and which eventually rang the death knell of Hitler's dream for a Nazi-controlled "fortress Europe." I even slid in a boastful reference to Dad's small role in the operation.

I honed my speech in the bathroom and my diligence paid off. My confidence started to soar, I shed my nervousness. I heard Gabby natter to Mom: *Tabernacle!* Somethin's got to be done about that limey accent, Flo."

The day of the speech went smoothly, though I had the strange sensation that my voice belonged to a stranger. My classmates were dumbstruck. Pete Riley slumped in his seat. D.D. scowled and tapped a pencil on his desk. When I finished there were snickers and a few claps. Sister St. Rose asked me to stay after class.

"That was quite a good speech you gave, Jim," she said when we were seated alone. "Congratulations."

"Thank you, Sister," I replied cheerily.

"Is your father English, Jim?" she asked politely.

"No, Sister. Irish."

"And your mother, then?"

"She's from Quebec."

"Well, then you must have spent time in England?"

"No, Sister," I said. "I've never been to the old sod."

"Of course, then you have an English nanny at home?"

"No, Sister. Just Gabby our housekeeper and she's French Canadian, like Mother."

There was a long pause. "I'm confused, Jim," she said at last. "Where did you get your English accent?"

I blushed scarlet. I got up to leave, tears in my eyes.

"I was just curious, that's all. One last thing," she said, as I was about to rush out the door. "Your father's Irish; I don't think he'd like your English accent. Remember, it's okay to just be yourself, Jim."

Part Three

FLYING HOME
THROUGH THE DARK

HE SEEMED LIKE
SOMEONE ELSE'S DAD

In December of 1944, I arrived home from school to find our place swarming with people. I heard the clink of glasses. Irv Pinkus met me in the front hall, clapped his big rough hand on my shoulder.

"Great news, Jimmy," he said. "I hear your dad's coming home."

Mom rushed down the hall, face wreathed in smiles, gave me a big hug. "Isn't it wonderful, son!" she said. "You'll be seeing your dad in a week or two."

The day of his arrival we got to the station in ample time, the train nowhere in sight. A crowd thronged the concrete platform, stamping their feet, cheeks pinched red by the cold air. I heard the faint clang of a bell, followed by a distant drawn-out whistle. Where the shining rails seemed to merge, a white light no bigger than a dot appeared. Pandemonium broke out. The engine's bell grew louder as the train crawled toward the station. A hush descended over the crowd. I felt the air vibrate as the train rumbled to a stop in front of us and everyone ran up and down the platform as the soldiers tumbled out of the side of the passenger cars onto the platform, brass buttons on their great coats gleaming, big grey duffel bags on their backs, whoops of joy rippling through the crowd. I heard Mom shout "It's him!" and saw her run toward a soldier I didn't recognize stepping down from the last car, kit bag slung over his shoulder. The stranger, who had a ruddy complexion and an ear-to-ear grin, bulked huge in his greatcoat. After Mom and the stranger hugged and kissed, he swung both my sisters into his arms, planted big kisses on their cheeks.

"What beautiful girls, Florie," he crooned, gazing proudly at them.

Gabby nudged me forward. "Just don't stand there," she ordered. "Give your daddy a big kiss."

The grinning soldier bent low and snatched me up in his powerful arms, his prickly whiskers scraping my cheeks. He seemed like someone else's dad, and when he set me down I stared at him, tongue-tied.

"He's grown into quite a little man," he said, patting my head.

"Well, aren't you going to tell your dad how happy you are to see him?" said Mom.

"I'm glad you're back home," I mumbled.

There was an afternoon welcome-home party at our tenement. Blue cigarette smoke choked the small rooms as friends squeezed together, drinking and laughing. Soon the hubbub became deafening, the smoke thicker, the kitchen table littered with empty beer bottles and spilt ashes. Peggy Hill, our pie-faced neighbour next door who was losing her hair and wore an ugly red turban, took my cheeks between her pudgy fingers, pinched and planted a fish-mouthed kiss on my lips, her blouse unbuttoned, beer on her breath.

"You must be very happy to have your dad back," she chirped. I didn't answer.

Peggy had a violent dislike of Irv from across the street because he was Jewish. She said things like "I got jewed." Once, during the war, we had run out of fuel and the coal company had refused to deliver. Mom had gone to Irv to ask for help and he had phoned the manager and blasted his callousness. "Shame on you!" he'd shouted. "This woman has three children and a husband overseas fighting for his country. Shame, shame on you!" and he had threatened that if something wasn't done right away he'd go to the authorities. That same afternoon, the coal truck backed up in our yard and our bin was filled to overflowing with glossy blueblack coal.

"Don't talk to me about the Jews," she'd say to Peggy. "If it hadn't been for Irv, we'd have all frozen to death."

As the afternoon wore on, Irv stood up on a chair, asked for quiet and proposed a toast. "To Sam," he said, raising his glass. "Thanks to men like him, we were able to stop that madman Hitler."

Everyone clinked glasses, and after the toast Irv added another, "And let's not forget Flo, who kept the home fires burning," and everybody cheered.

Dad turned into his old gregarious self, showing everyone the horizontal scar across his right cheek and side of his neck where the sniper bullet had pierced his earlobe.

"Another quarter inch," he said, "and I'd have been a goner."

I avoided Dad as much as I could, content to watch from a distance, trying to figure out who this stranger was with the friendly smile and husky voice, the one who laughed and drank and shouted, and who sang off-key and banged his fist on the kitchen table. Who was the soldier who told me to call him "Dad," who said he loved me, wanted me to love him, too, a stranger with hairy hands and a dry kiss? Who was this soldier? I resented it when he parked his kit bag and greatcoat in Mom's bedroom.

MY SISTERS AND I
EXCHANGED GLANCES MUTELY,
BUT DID NOT MOVE

When Dad was still in Kingston waiting for his official discharge, my sister Babe, who had been playing in the summer kitchen, accidentally crushed the sound box of Gabby's Hawaiian guitar that had been gathering dust for months in a corner. Gabby flew into a rage and with a vicious twist to her face threatened to lock Babe in the cellar.

I yelled at Gabby, telling her to stop. She whacked me across the back hard with her switch. When I tried to run she slashed my back twice more, drawing blood. That evening, when Mom got home, I did something I'd never done before: I showed her the purplish welts on my back. Mom turned white with fury. From upstairs, I could hear Cherie yelping amidst a flurry of angry words. I looked through the stovepipe hole in the floor just as Mom slapped Gabby's face, bloodying her lower lip. I remember Gabby's hysterical sobbing, a door slamming shut, and then a silence.

Mom came to my bedroom, examined my back, and rubbed zinc ointment over the welts. She was breathing heavily. Tears rolled down her face, all I could hear was her muffled gasps. "I'm very, very sorry, son. I've let you and your sisters down badly. This will never happen again, I promise."

The following Saturday, suitcases packed, Cherie in her arms, Gabby got into a taxi that took her to the CPR station for the train back to Quebec. The evening after Gabby's departure, during what was our usual curfew, Mom told us we could go out and play. My sisters and I exchanged glances mutely, but did not move, tongues stuck to the roof of our mouths till the realization sank in: Gabby was no longer in charge. Letting out loud whoops, we dashed out the door to our newfound freedom. A few weeks later, I chanced upon Gabby's Westclox on a shelf in the summer kitchen and hammered it to smithereens in the backyard, burying the pieces in the same hole I'd dug for Jack's booze. I never saw Gabby again. According to the family grapevine, she ended up in a psychiatric institution where she died in her early 50s. I never did find out what happened to my old nemesis, Adrian.

Dad came home irregularly on leave. He and Mom would go to the beer parlour on Saturday afternoons that for me were edged with menace. They would park me and my sisters in the lobby. Every time the parlour door opened, releasing stale beery air, I would glance up hoping it was them. Strangers were always touching us. They would lurch past, pat our heads and tell us, "Be good, children." Bored and uneasy, I would sneak outside to the Otonabee to watch the grey glide of the river water, to listen to the wind whooshing in the willows along the banks as the late after-noon sun crept over the tenements on Water Street, a movement of shadows that would calm me.

One weekend when Dad was home, he took some war trophies out of his kit bag: a green cloth flak badge displaying an 88 gun nestled in wings inside a wreath that had a small swastika at the bottom, and a metal German Hitler Youth badge with a larger black swastika against a cream-coloured enamel field.

He wouldn't let me handle them. "They're not toys," he said, and was careful to put them back in his bag. That same weekend he had Myles Gorman and Pat O'Hara, his two buddies, over and, as they were drinking and chatting about the war in the parlour (something Dad rarely did), I was in the kitchen and eavesdropped on their conversation.

"Normandy was no picnic," Dad was saying. "The Germans fought to the last. The Hitler Youth in particular were fanatical. They would die rather than surrender. It was too bad. Mere lads they were, some only 14 or 15, not much older than my Jimmy."

When Dad came into the kitchen to fetch more beer from the icebox, my presence startled him, he seemed upset.

"What's ya doing in the house, lad?" he barked. "Get out and play!"

I did as I was told.

The firemen had a shooting range on the south side of the fire hall basement where they practiced target shooting and some of the local police tested their weapons. The room, which was long and narrow, was kept locked and had walls of concrete and stone and a pile of sandbags at the target end. Not long after Dad showed me his trophies, Josh and I were at the hall when Vic Rome, the electrician, produced a German luger and invited us to try it, to our delight. After he cautioned us about the kickback and how to grip the weapon with both hands, he let us fire off a couple of rounds. Our glee knew no bounds.

Tuesday May 8th 1945, after morning recess, we formed columns of three in the basement of our school to begin the long march up the staircase back to our classrooms. Under the scrutiny of Sister Luke, we stomped up the stairs as the music teacher, Sister Roberta, pounded out "The Battle Hymn of the Republic" on the piano. Suddenly, we heard cannons boom from the downtown armouries and church bells began to peal throughout the city. Factory whistles screeched. A few minute later, just as we finished singing the Marian hymn, "O Mary we crown thee with roses today, Queen of the Angels, Queen of the May," Sister Luke swept into our classroom and announced that the war in Europe was over and that school was cancelled for the rest of the day. We whooped and cheered and swarmed out the doors.

I ran downtown. Horns shrilled, ribbons of ticker tape and toilet paper floated down on the jubilant crowd from the upper windows of buildings, a loudspeaker blared "When Johnny Comes Marching Home Again," and strangers embraced each other and kissed, linked arms and whirled in circles in the middle of the street. Liquor flowed.

Everyone, it seemed, had a bottle. The terrible pall that had hung over the city for years had suddenly lifted.

I spent that afternoon and most of the evening downtown. I clambered across the rooftops of the downtown buildings, hurling reams of toilet paper and balloons laden with water on the crowd below. From my rooftop vantage point I spotted Alice and Ollie Riley, Pete's parents, on the sidewalk below and tried to water bomb their hoity-toity heads, but missed. Some of my doused victims glanced up, shook fists in mock anger, but most didn't care. It was as though a champagne cork had been pulled, releasing six years of pent-up emotion. The euphoria couldn't be contained.

Truth be told, the battle against the Axis was far from over as greater horrors loomed ahead. On the 6th of August, 1945, the Americans dropped "Little Boy," the first atomic bomb, on Hiroshima, followed by the dropping of a second bomb, "Fat Man," three days later on Nagasaki. Newsreels showed mushroom clouds as they turned into dark toxic blooms. I was appalled by the blasted landscapes caused by the shocking new weapon and for a long time the spectre of a blackened single tree etched against an empty sky at Hiroshima stalked my dreaming and waking moments.

But that day in May, when I returned home and tumbled into bed, I wasn't thinking of the total victory that was to come. I was so exhilarated I couldn't sleep. The words of Sister Luke: "The war in Europe is finally over" kept drumming in my ears and all I could think of was Dad finally coming home and all of us living together in our new dream house.

Discharged in May, he was hired back as a waiter at the Empress Hotel. A few weeks after VE Day, when I thought he was still at work, I tiptoed into his bedroom and fished out his German souvenirs from the kit bag and brandished them before my friends in the York Trading yard, spinning a tall tale about how he had killed dozens of fanatical Hitler Youth with a bayonet in hand-to-hand combat. Dad, who had been at the fire hall, overheard the boasting and bolted out from behind the fire hall lane fence, furious. He boxed my ears.

"Don't ya ever talk like that again, lad!" he shouted, eyes blazing. "And what's this I hear about you and Josh firing a luger? If you ever do that again I'll do ya. Do ya hear me, lad? I'll do ya!"

He stormed into the tenement, slamming the back door behind him. Dad must have spoken to Josh's father for next evening, when I was at the front of the fire hall talking to one of the men, the rabbi beckoned from across the street. In a truculent voice he put me on notice that under no circumstances was his son Josh ever to fire a handgun in the station again, especially a German luger or he would speak to the Chief personally. I squirmed as his sad Talmudic eyes never strayed from my face, pinned me with guilt. "I hope I've made myself clear, young man. As Fire Mascot, I'm holding you responsible," he added.

I never touched Dad's medals or entered the shooting range again.

SKIRMISHES

Dad brought home a dog he had picked up at the pound, a small white puppy, part pit bull, part god-knows-what else, a gift for me (my sisters liked cats), and I called him Laddie.

Laddie had a wide powerful muzzle and grew into a short, powerfully muscled animal who was friendly and affectionate around the house, but raised his hackles when other dogs strayed near. He particularly bristled when Ebony, Old Irish's shaggy black collie-cum-terrier mutt from across the street, sniffed around. The dogs bared fangs and snarled at each other when they met and had to be kept apart. Ebony was taller and slightly heavier than Laddie and Old Irish seemed to relish their fierce skirmishes. Dad warned me never to allow Laddie off the leash when Ebony was around.

One December morning, close to my birthday, I was upstairs in my bedroom when I awakened to Shirl's shout: "The dogs are loose!"

I raced out the front door. It had snowed the night before and Simcoe Street was layered white. On opposite sides of the street Laddie and Ebony paced back and forth, growling and barking. I could hear Old Irish standing in his doorway prodding his dog to "Gettum, Ebony! Gettum!"

The dogs shot toward each other, and clashed and reared on hind legs in the middle of the road, beginning a terrible dance, spittle flying, their growls fierce, pawing and snapping at each other. The dogs tumbled on their sides and Ebony broke free, dove back clamping on to Laddie by the back of his head. Laddie jiggered, arched his back, trying to loosen Ebony's jaw. Ebony yanked Laddie up and whipped his head down hard on the snow-covered pavement, his hind legs splaying. But the taller dog lost his grip and Laddie twisted his trunk around, swivelled on his backbone, back legs churning the air, and sunk his fangs into Ebony's throat.

As Laddie ground down, working his jaws, deepening and widening the wound in Ebony's throat, more blood spurted from his neck. Dad rushed out and he and Old Irish grabbed both dogs by the scruff of their necks. Dad was able to pry open Laddie's jaw with a stick.

Ebony survived the encounter. Old Irish lost his lust for dog fights. Dad blamed me. "You lost control of your dog, lad," he said. I remember that day as the time when all the white snow turned to scarlet tears.

ANGRIER THAN I'D EVER
SEEN HIM BEFORE

For four or five years I delivered the *Examiner*, the local paper, fair weather, foul weather, door-to-door, six days a week to about 50 subscribers, mostly in the downtown, and I took my job seriously. The company supplied us with a paper bag and I folded the paper in thirds or fifths depending on the thickness of that day's edition so that I could toss the newspaper at a door or verandah while riding my bike on the sidewalk. I became expert at plopping the newspaper on the customer's doorsill out of reach of snow or rain. In winter, it often took the horse-drawn ploughs more than a day to clear the sidewalks and I would haul my newspapers on my small wooden sleigh. If the weather was biting cold, I wore two scarves, one around my neck, the other wrapped over my face and tied behind the head. I still hear the soggy hum of tires on wet asphalt in the summer and the crackle of their chains in icy weather.

The paper held regular circulation contests, and the year after Dad came home from the War I was one of the winners of a weekend trip to Rochester, New York. We embarked on the big white ferry, *SS Ontario # 1*, at

Cobourg. In my youthful imagination, never having ventured far from Simcoe Street, the trip across sun-silvered Lake Ontario was like crossing the Atlantic. After the drab war years when electricity was rationed and signs blackened out, the neon splendour of downtown Rochester dazzled me and made me feel as if I had entered a new fairy-tale world. But most thrilling of all were the Dick Tracey cap guns we bought, silver .45s, with their spools of caps, narrow red paper strips with powder bumps that fitted into the handle and went "Bang! Bang!" when you squeezed the trigger, just like in the gangster movies. On the way home we chased one another all over the boat, playing soldiers and cops and robbers, firing caps at each other, dropping to the deck and pretending to be mortally wounded when someone scored a direct hit.

Cruel fantasies jumped into my skin. Using the savings I had banked as a paperboy (one of the benefits of the job was thriftiness), I bought a BB gun, a Daisy single-shot rifle, and set out on a rampage of wanton and indiscriminate destruction – shooting birds, chipmunks, squirrels, frogs, almost anything that moved. At Jackson's Park, I'd target frogs, big, plump, noisy bullfrogs as they sunned themselves on the smooth, sun-baked rocks. I pretended they were Japs and thrilled to watch them hurtle high in the air and flip-flop on their backs, goggle-eyed, the brass pellet bulging like a piece of shrapnel from their creamy chests.

One bright July afternoon in the backyard of the tenement, Peggy, our twitchy disagreeable neighbour, caught me red-handed picking off grackles, *ping-ping-ping*, as they alighted on the branches of the maple. In my eyes they were hated German warplanes and I rejoiced as the stricken birds tumbled through the rustling foliage to the ground, their black feathers splayed scarlet. Peggy threatened to phone the police but, instead, blabbed to Dad.

Dad surveyed the red carpet of dead birds on the ground, at first stupefied and grim, then flushed with anger, angrier than I'd ever seen him before. He made me pick up the birds lying on their backs, little twig legs sticking straight in the air, dig a hole and bury them in a cardboard box in the backyard. Picking up their bodies sent shivers of guilt through my flesh. Then he found my BB gun in the summer kitchen, took the axe from the shed, and smashed it. He threw the pieces at my feet. "Don't let me catch you killing birds again," he roared, "or I'll do ya, lad. I promise!"

I never hunted again.

THE SMASHING OF HER DREAM

I heard an angry commotion in the kitchen. I peered into the old upstairs chimney hole in the cold linoleum floor. Mom was pacing to and fro in her blue housecoat, fists on her hips, one holding a balled-up handkerchief. She was sobbing.

"How could you have, Sam?" Dad sat mute on a chair, hands covering his face. Then he rose, knocked over his chair, stumbled out of the kitchen, slamming their bedroom door. Mom picked up the toppled chair and sat at the table, laid her head on her folded arms and wept softly. I climbed back into bed and gazed at the grainy autumn light in the window. Mom's weeping seeped into my bones. The next day I learned that Dad had gambled away his gratuity, the nest egg Mom had counted on for a down payment on their new home, lost in one all-night session of poker. For the first time in my life I felt the fire of impotent rage.

Mom never forgave Dad for the loss of the gratuity, the smashing of her dream. Over the years she would gnaw on her disappointment like an old bone, and anytime they drank together she would bring the subject up, rancorous words volleying back and forth across the kitchen table. I learned the art of strategic withdrawal. My clothes closet became my foxhole in a combat zone, a place where I could catch my breath, despite the thunder of the guns.

Other times during their skirmishes, I would slip outside into the yard and gaze at the shimmering stars, dumbfounded by the universe, how I'd just recently learned our sun is among 200 billion suns in the Milky Way, which in turn is only one of millions of galaxies, each moving away from the others at 1000 miles a second, their light moving through space like a long late train. I recall seeing the sky as a field of molten stars and suddenly I was seized by a sense of God's presence. I ran to the nearest maple and threw my arms around its trunk, calmed and comforted, as though the tree were divine energy lifting the gloom from my soul.

Around Christmas of that first year, Mom dispatched me to the Johnson House, a popular drinking hole known as the Pig's Ear, to bring Dad home.

"Hurry, Jim," she said. "The hotel's just phoned and said he's in bad shape."

It had snowed heavily and the sidewalks were clogged with snow. As I waded through the snowdrifts, I heard the strains of "Silent Night" and glimpsed a small Salvation Army band in a cone of streetlight streaked with blowing snow at the corner of Aylmer and Hunter Streets. When I finally got to the hotel, the dark, cavernous beverage room was almost deserted.

"Looking for Sam, son?" the bartender asked, nodding toward the back. "He's over there, but you're too young to be in here."

"But Mom sent me to help him home."

He glanced once more in Dad's direction, then said, "Okay, son, this time, but make it quick."

I groped through the maze of chairs and tables and spotted Dad slumped at a table, staring at the floor, mumbling to himself. I tapped his shoulder.

"It's me, Dad, Jim, here to take you home."

He looked pasty-white in the dim light. I cajoled him into leaving and, supporting his arm, walked him home through the snow.

The next day, Dr. O'Brien warned him that his liver was shot. He would have to give up alcohol or he'd be pushing up daisies within two years. But he paid no attention: "I'll dance on your grave, Florie."

THE BOOZE AND MUSIC
MELTED HEARTS

When Dad and Mom fell off the wagon our tenement, it seemed, became something of an oasis for every alcoholic acquaintance in town (and sometimes complete strangers) who would drift in to quaff a drink or two and spend a few hours forgetting their woes.

On St. Patrick's Day, Dad invited all his Irish cronies to the house to celebrate, North and South alike, it didn't matter. Myles Gorman, the taxi man, would always be one of the first to arrive with a bottle of Bushmill's Irish whiskey tucked in his arms. Pat O' Hara, who worked with Dad at the hotel, would bring his guitar, and Michael Brown, once the town's leading advocate, always appeared spiffed-up in a blue pinstriped suit, immaculate white shirt and a fancy tie. One time he got Mom's dander up by rolling up his pant cuffs. "Your floors are dusty, Flo." (Brown, whose wife eventually took their children and left, predicted that one day I would become a lawyer, just like him, but his excessive tippling eventually led to his disbarment. Years later, Mom read of his demise in the *Toronto Star.* The police, it was reported, had discovered his emaciated body in a

Cabbagetown flophouse, dead two weeks, an empty bottle of Four Aces on the bed beside him.)

As the party rollicked on and became more maudlin, Pat, strumming his guitar, would warble "A Teardrop on a Rose," one of Hank Williams' big hits:

> *While strolling through a lovely garden*
> *As day was drawing to a close*
> *My eyes beheld a tragic story*
> *I saw a teardrop on a rose.*

Dad would dragoon Shirl into playing the piano. The celebration would sink into a bog of Irish bathos. When Babe sang one of Dad's favourites, "I'll Take You Home Again, Kathleen," his eyes would dim with tears and he, for some unknown reason, would reel off the titles of all the books of the Old Testament, learned by heart in Sunday school during his strict Protestant upbringing: Genesis, Exodus, Leviticus, Numbers, Deuteronomy, Joshua... all coming trippingly off his tongue in a cascade of slurry syllables, never missing a book. Afterwards, at some mysterious but luminous moment, a hush would fall over the room, and clasping a glass of Bushmill's Dad would position himself, gaze heavenward, and in a tuneless baritone belt out (though croak would be more accurate) his favourite song, "Danny Boy," accompanied by hand gestures and crocodile tears. As Myles, immersed in memories of his dead mother, wept copiously, Dad would pluck his own mother's portrait off the wall and press it fervently to his breast. By early evening everyone was either barely mobile or passed out, snoring loudly.

On one occasion, Dad hauled me across the street to pray for Kathleen, Old Irish O' Sullivan's ailing wife. She was grieving the loss of her son Martin (Young Irish) the gambler, who had died a year earlier of heart seizure. We found Kathleen in bed in her filthy nightgown on sheets speckled with stains, eyes half shut, skin the colour of chalk. The bedroom reeked of urine and whiskey. A crucifix hung on the wall above the bed and a half-empty bottle of Johnny Walker sat on the dresser. On another wall, a fair-haired Jesus, clutching his own red pierced heart, looked down on us. Dad ordered me to kneel down beside the bed and pray for the old lady in Latin. I declaimed with gusto the *Confiteor*, while Old Irish, stubble-bearded, looked on, shaking his head, tears pouring down his face. After I finished, Dad exclaimed: "I told ya, Sullie, the lad's a wizard in Latin."

The St. Patrick's Day party proved a bonanza for my sisters and me in more tangible ways. The nostalgia generated by the booze and music melted hearts and everyone became exceedingly generous, which translated into big tips for us. Someone would slip me a two- or five-dollar bill to buy cigarettes or cigars at the corner store, and when I got back they would tell me to keep the change. Often bills or loose change would accidentally spill on the floor, which we would treat as treasure trove and stuff in our pockets.

Myles always parked his blue four-door Chevrolet taxi at the curb in front of the tenement. It had a vertical chrome strip that bisected the windscreen. Myles was very fastidious about the car, but when he was three sheets to the wind he would let me mount the running board to mimic G-men, Tommy guns blazing at bootleggers just like in the movies. Sometimes he would allow me to sit behind the wheel, my sisters in the back, and explain the rudiments of driving, how to work the gears, etc. I still recall the prickle of the stiff mouldy-smelling upholstery on my skin and the cool smooth feel of the blue knob at the end of the gearstick. Occasionally, if he was feeling especially indulgent, Myles would take us for a spin in the car around the block. A ride in an automobile was a major event in our lives and we would get so excited that we would race into the house afterwards yelling our heads off and talk about the ride to our friends for days. Mom pegged Myles as a cheapskate. "Considering the free booze he guzzles around here," she'd say, "you'd think he'd give us a free ride now and again. But he never does."

A healing quietness had settled over the tenement. I tiptoed downstairs to empty beer bottles everywhere, cigarette burns on the kitchen oilcloth, glasses and dirty dishes on the counter and in the sink. The linoleum chilled the soles of my feet. .

At 7 a.m., Mom's Black Forest parlour clock chimed its notes sharp as glass in the stillness. Someone in the downstairs bedroom stirred. I eased open the door. Dad was snoring quietly on his side of the bed, naked, lips slightly apart; Mom's white slip was rumpled above her waist, exposing her white thighs and her nest of dark hair. I recoiled and ran back upstairs, crawled under the sheets, my whole body shivering.

THE GREEN HORNET

One April afternoon, Dad came home from the hotel to announce that he had been fired. Mom was crushed: the loss of the gratuity and her dream home and now this, three young children to care for, and an unemployed husband who, as the weeks dragged on, went deeper into the drink. Mom announced she was going to talk to Colonel Cooper, the manager at Hydro. He had been Dad's commanding officer overseas with the SD and G's and, like Dad, had been wounded at Caen. "If he can't help us, no one can." Two hours later she returned, a big smile on her face.

"Guess what, Sam," she said. "You've now got a new job. Next Monday you'll be starting at the Hydro!" She quoted Colonel Cooper: "If a veteran with a wife and three kids who risked his life for his country doesn't deserve a job, nobody does."

In August, Dad told us that we were going to visit the Thompsons on the farm in Bobcaygeon, "Ma" and "Pa" as he called them, even though he had neither seen nor contacted them in years.

"Pat O' Hara will drive us up." He bought Ma and Pa a fancy china dinner plate imprinted with a pair of Belgians. "They love horses."

Early one Saturday morning toward the end of August, the day of the visit, Pat drove a 1939 green Ford sedan, a rusted-out jalopy that we called The Green Hornet. It was on its last legs, rust showing on its big round fenders, and there were holes in the running boards. Mom, who was leery about the trip, especially with Pat driving, had dressed us all up for the occasion, including a new white shirt and freshly pressed trousers for Dad. While Mom hustled about getting us ready, Pat produced a bottle of Seagram's, sat down with Dad in the parlour and, as they had a "wee one for the road," Pat strummed his guitar and sang "Lovesick Blues," a popular Hank Williams tune:

> *I got a feelin' called the blu-ues, oh Lawd*
> *Since my baby said good-bye....*

We jammed into The Green Hornet, with me and my sisters and the guitar scrunched in the back. The jalopy lurched forward and Mom said: "Don't drink any more, Sam." In the dome of sky, there wasn't a single small cloud.

We had only travelled a few miles on the Lindsay highway when Dad and Pat began swigging straight from the bottle. "Don't worry, lad," Dad told us. "Pat's a good driver."

All the way to Lindsay Dad rhapsodized about the four years he had worked on the Thompson farm, how Ma and Pa had treated him like a son, how he ploughed the fields with Pete and Bess, the team of Belgians, and milked the dairy herd by hand, forked manure and bucked hay in the barn. There were tears in his eyes. "You grow up fast on a farm."

When we got to Lindsay, Pat claimed to know the town like the back of his hand. He got lost, ran a red light, and made such a screeching U-turn off the main street that it felt like The Green Hornet was going to tumble on its side. We ended up straddling both the railway tracks and roadway, one side of the car bumping over the ties, thump, thump, thump, unable to get off the tracks and out of danger till we reached the next intersection. After blundering down several wrong roads, Pat found the right direction to Bobcaygeon and we barrelled over more pitted and winding back roads, past lacklustre farms, with Dad mumbling incoherent directions till at last we arrived.

Ma and Pa, a nice elderly couple with white hair, gave my sisters and me milk and cookies. Dad took us into the barnyard and tried to show us how to catch a pig barehanded and tumbled headfirst into the muck. In the enormous barn, slivers of sunlight sliced the gloom, wind whistled in the chinks as we watched Dad, high up the hayloft ladder. "I'll show ya how it's done, lad!" he yelled, just as he slipped and crashed to the floorboards, the good white shirt Mom had bought for the trip soiled and torn. A worried Ma and Pa urged us to stay the night but Pat and Dad insisted they were in good shape and had to get back. Dad remembered the gift and fetched it from the car. As he crossed the kitchen threshold, he stumbled and fell, smashing the plate to pieces.

Back on the road, The Green Hornet lurched and wove down the highway. Pat and Dad continued to swig from the bottle. The windshield popped open. The wind shrieked. Oncoming traffic honked and swerved, flashing their brights at us. My sisters and I complained that we had to pee. Pat pulled over beside a small wood. The sun had almost set. Sweat was dripping from my face, my sisters' rosy complexions turned the colour of mushrooms. When we crammed back into The Green Hornet we found Pat and Dad in the back seat, snoring, Pat's guitar crushed. We shouted. We shook their shoulders. They were both dead to the world. I closed my eyes, mumbled a quick Hail Mary, got into the driver's seat, switched on the ignition, and gripping the wheel, my knuckles white as bone, shifted gears and stamped on the gas pedal. The Green Hornet bounced back onto the highway and flew home through the dark.

For weeks, the same nightmare plagued me: our house was an old runaway car with my sisters in the back seat and no driver behind the wheel as we rattled and wheezed down a dark road toward an invisible high cliff.

EYES GLAZED, GAIT WOBBLY

The Montreal House, not far from the Hydro yard, became Dad's drinking hole: at noon, beer (four or five "chasers," as he called them) and, after work, a half-dozen more before he made his tangle-footed way home for supper — usually with one or two bottles of Catawba or Four Aces (the cheapest "sherry" in the liquor store) cradled in his arm. I don't recall a family meal with him present. He always ate alone or, occasionally, with Mom, the kitchen filled with the smell of pork hocks and boiled potatoes or cabbage, or whatever favourite dish he was preparing, and by 9 p.m. he would have downed another full bottle of sherry and would be in bed, snoring. In the morning, before leaving for work, he would guzzle back another bottle of sherry. The floor of the summer kitchen was so littered with empty bottles Mom would only put out the empty bottles in small batches on garbage days. "I don't want the neighbours to think we're bootleggers."

I had learned to play pool on the table in the recreation room at the fire hall and at Spiro's poolroom on Charlotte Street. There were billiard tables at the Empress and I had heard stories about Dad's prowess at the table.

"At one time your dad was one of the best English billiard players in the city," Mom told me.

He challenged me to a game of snooker at Spiro's. "We'll see who's the best man, lad," he said. The afternoon of the match, he showed up, eyes glazed, gait unsteady. He miscued several times and once, in frustration, banged his cue against the edge of the table. I beat him two games in a row. When I asked if he wanted a third game he threw down his cue and stormed out.

Babe had been dating the Booth boy on Bethune Street. Babe was a gifted student and the nuns had complained that her schoolwork had fallen off. Dad blamed the Booth boy. One evening, Babe came home well beyond curfew and tried to sneak into bed through her bedroom window by climbing onto the tin roof of the woodshed. She fell halfway through the roof. Dad rushed into the shed to find her legs dangling in mid-air. He called her "a whore" and took off his belt. As he was about to lash her legs, I grabbed his arm: "Hit her and I'll kill you!"

Dad glared at me. He stomped back to his bedroom, spluttering.

The next day, when I got home from school, I could tell he was itching to fight.

"So you think you're a man?" he said, tucking his chin and clenching his fist. "I'll teach ya." He slammed his fist into my sternum, sending me flying backwards over the chesterfield.

"Get up, ya Fenian, and fight like a man!" When I tried to rise he slugged me again, harder. I was 16 and weighed

175 pounds, awkward, but strong. When he cocked his fist again, I beat him to the punch, hitting him solidly on the chest. My punch only inflamed him. We grappled, lurching and banging down the hallway till we came to the bedroom door and fell onto the bed. Our eyes locked as we lay face to face, the closest we ever got. Out of pure exhaustion we ceased struggling. Neither of us ever mentioned the fight again. I remember it with shame.

FLORIE, LET ME IN!

In high school I became so focused on sports and morbidly conscious of girls — I'd cross the street to avoid their gaze — I spent less and less time at the fire hall. I also became aware of social distinctions and the world beyond Simcoe Street. I developed a fascination with the big homes of my well-to-do friends in the west end. Whenever I got the chance, I'd stroll through the shady cool streets, marvelling at the beauty of quiet crew-cut lawns, the wrap-around verandahs, the shiny new cars in the driveways. I'd stop and gaze through their huge front windows, wondering who these people were who lived in such elegance, dined together in candle-lit splendour. They seemed a race apart. Was this the normal way families lived? And what was normal anyway? I grew ashamed of our shabby tenement and my parents' drinking. If anyone offered me a drive home after school or some event, I would either politely decline or, if I did accept, insist that I be dropped off a block or two from the tenement and would trot out some spurious excuse that I had to meet someone or run an errand. The thought of anyone knowing where I lived was unbearable. I also grieved the warm camaraderie some of my friends had with their dads.

I urged Mom to move. "We may not be able to buy a house, but we can rent a better place than this dismal dump." Mom and I began to scan the local papers for rentals and to follow up on leads. We knew that if Dad discovered what we were up to he would try to scupper our plans. Our only hope was a *fait accompli*.

One afternoon, we found a decent, affordable apartment near the downtown with three bedrooms, central heating, burnished hardwood floors and a lovely mahogany fireplace surmounted by a bevelled mirror – undreamt of luxury. Mr. Wilson, the landlord, offered to rent it to us. He seemed impressed that Mom and Dad had steady jobs and that I was doing well at school. We were overjoyed.

It had started to rain. We reluctantly accepted the landlord's offer of a drive home. As his car rolled to a stop in front of the tenement, Mom and I caught sight of Dad rounding the corner, a bottle tucked in the crook of his arm, lurching from side to side, stumbling to the front door where he found it locked. He yelled: "Florie, let me in!" Getting no response, he kicked out the pane of the ground-floor bedroom window and clambered through the jagged hole, still clutching the bottle, and fell headlong into the room. Mom and I were aghast.

We had not been in the house fifteen minutes before the phone rang. It was Mr. Wilson. "I'm terribly sorry," he said, "but my wife reminded me when I got home that the apartment had already been spoken for." The look of grim resignation on Mom's pale stricken face pushed me to the verge of tears. Another of her hopes sputtered out. It seemed that life on Simcoe Street was a game of chutes and ladders, mostly chutes. Gabby and Mom were right: life isn't fair.

A few weeks later, I dreamt I was living in a decrepit tenement, grimy and uninhabitable where the wind sifted through the thin walls of my bedroom, ruffling the loose floral wallpaper. I took refuge in a closet where I discovered a secret door that led up a winding staircase to a beautiful tropical garden, an oasis in the desert, a place of light and refreshment, filled with fragrant exotic flowers. A sickle moon hung on the pale-blue morning horizon. A man approached and I asked him the age of the tenement.

"Ancient," he said, and I felt a deep peace.

NOT EVEN A POSTCARD

One Saturday in late fall, I had spent most of the day on George Street downtown watching the firemen fight a blaze. The fire had started in a third-floor apartment above a Chinese restaurant where the owner of the restaurant was sleeping. He had made it to the front window, kicked out the glass, and leapt only seconds before the firemen had their net ready.

Rushed by ambulance to St. Joseph's Hospital, the man died on the operating table. Back at the fire hall, I watched the blackened faces of the men as they straggled into the station, mouths pinched with fatigue. As they strung up the wet hoses in the dry tower, a pall of defeat hung over the fire hall. I knew they took any death on their watch personally and I felt pity, not only for the victim but for them, too.

When I got home that evening, Mom and Dad were in the kitchen, a half-empty bottle of Seagram's on the kitchen table between them. We chatted about the fire and the tragic loss of life, but, as usual when she drank, a familiar scenario unfolded: Mom became sentimental and began to tell me how much she loved "your daddy" and vowed he had always been the love of her life. Then, stroking his cheek, she'd sing:

Come to me my melancholy baby,
Cuddle up and don't be blue...
All your fears are foolish fancy, maybe
You know, dear, that I'm in love with you.

Every cloud must have a silver lining
Wait until the sun shines through
Smile my honey dear, while I kiss away each tear
Or else I shall be melancholy too.

Then, her jaw would lock and she would begin to slur her words, a cigarette dangling from her lips, as the powerful undertow of past hurts and disappointments pulled her downward. After a time, her jaw would unlock and she would start dredging up all her grievances that went back to the earliest days of their marriage: the night she came home with me from the hospital in a taxi around Christmas to find Dad and Old Irish in the kitchen, plastered, a gallon of red wine on the table, and his callous answer when she asked if he'd bought her flowers: "I gave you a beautiful son, didn't I?" The time after their wedding, when he forbad her tell anyone at the hotel they were married, and took a two-month solitary honeymoon to Belfast and returned with three Yorkie pups for the Grahams, the owners of the hotel, but nothing for her. "Not even a postcard," she said. And the dreary litany went on and on. When Dad protested, as he invariably did: "Let bygones be bygones, Florie," she would break into song:

> *Who's sorry now*
> *Who's sorry now*
> *Whose heart is achin' for breakin' each vow*
> *Who's sad and blue, who's cryin' too*
> *Just like I cried over you*
>
> *Right to the end*
> *Just like a friend*
> *I tried to warn you somehow*
> *You had your way*
> *Now you must pay*
> *I'm glad that you're sorry now.*

Dad would retreat to the bedroom, and I would escape upstairs to my room and hole up in the cramped stuffy closet that I had rigged up with table and lamp so that I could shut the door against the bedlam of the house.

"But I want you to stay," she said on the night of the fire.

"Sorry, Mom, I've got homework." I could see that she felt betrayed.

I had other hidey-holes where I could cancel out the world and the people around me. Sometimes I would go the Columbus Hall down the street and install myself in the ballroom upstairs, a quiet place, especially on Sundays, and imagine ghostly dancers whirling around to the mellow music of Del Crary and his orchestra, till the big silver clock over the bandstand told me it was safe to return home. Or if the day was sunny and warm, I would hike out the rails to Jackson's Point, lie on a carpet of needles, watch the sunlight dappling the pine tops, listen to the splash of the shallow brown creek, and let the sifting of the wind for a few stolen moments lull me into forgetfulness, permit me to feel light and invisible.

But that evening I was upset and could not stop thinking of the fire downtown, the man leaping from the window, the desolate look on the firemen's faces back at the fire hall. I dozed off on the bed only to be awakened by the murmur of voices in the kitchen. I looked down the chimney hole to see Mom handing cash to Ruby the bootlegger, a middle-aged blonde with smooth skin and a high-pitched voice. She reached into her big purse and pulled out a bottle of rye, set it on the table and, as though following a well-rehearsed script, stuck around, looking pale and thirsty till Dad, who had re-emerged from the bedroom, offered her a drink. Then, as the bantering and laughing tossed back and forth, I waited for Mom to deliver her highest compliment: "Ruby, what's a woman like you doing in this business?" which never failed to bring a tear to Ruby's eye.

I nodded off again, but was startled awake by Mom standing near my bed, fists on her hips. I felt a sharp blow to my face. "The next time I ask you to stay, you stay," she snarled and left.

Next morning, foraging in the kitchen, Dad lamented, "Florie, Ruby drank all our booze again."

When Mom came into the kitchen, puffy-eyed, and saw me sitting at the kitchen table, she recoiled, horror in her eyes.

"*Oeil au beurre!*" she cried, "I didn't do that, did I?"

I rose, looked into the kitchen mirror and saw a purplish bruise around my right eye. I chose not to answer her, concerned only about how I would explain a black eye to my schoolmates.

WITH A SCREAM IN MY HEART

Frederick Buechner wrote that God makes himself powerfully and personally known to us through our stories. Laying bare our lives offers all of us the opportunity for introspection. It reassures us we are not alone. We do not "have" secrets, we "are" our secrets, he says, and to trust each other enough to share them has much to do with the secret of what it means to be human.

To see Mom drinking was profoundly disturbing to me as a child. Because Dad had abdicated his role as father, Mom had become the central figure in our lives, the engine that kept our little plane flying. My sisters and I had learned how to navigate around Dad's drinking and had found ways to carry on as though he didn't exist. As long as Mom was captain, our family could fly, just like returning Lancaster bombers in the movies, on one parental engine. But when all the engines conked out, we knew serious danger was lurking, that our little craft was headed for disaster.

Oh, the crushing feeling of helplessness and panic to see Mom wandering woozily around the house, leaving a trail of ashes behind her in a haze of blue smoke, her white slip soiled, eyes puffy, hair unkempt; she who was normally so meticulous about her appearance. In the miasma created by alcohol she became bellicose, and turned on Dad, trotting out in lurid detail (Mom had a remarkable memory) all his infidelities, his broken promises, the loss of her dream house. Her list went on and on until he would finally decide he'd had enough. My gaze would turn to the squirming flies on the yellow flypaper near the stove. I knew what was coming next: he would snatch his bottle and leave, sometimes clacking the kitchen door so hard I thought the flies would shudder loose, but they never did.

If there was no food in the house, Mom would slip us a few dollars and send us to the Boston Café on Charlotte Street, a small Chinese eatery that had wooden booths with high backs, and where, for 75 cents each, we could get a three-course dinner. We craved the balm of Mom's attention, but no strategies we could devise could sway her from her obsession with Dad's foibles. An emptiness gaped in the pit of our stomachs, widening and widening till it threatened to swallow us all.

In the morning, the acrid smell of tobacco penetrated every room in the house, infested our clothes, and stung my eyes, often leaving me with a constricted chest and sore throat. The stench from overflowing ashtrays made me nauseous. We would find ragged black-edged holes in the oilcloth on the kitchen table and scorch marks on the furniture. My sisters and I had to be constantly on the lookout for telltale signs of smoke for we were afraid she might accidentally set fire to the tenement and kill us all. Once, I discovered a burn hole in her bedroom mattress the size of a golf ball, and twice I found her passed out on the floor in the hallway, clothes dishevelled and breast and pubic hair exposed. When I tried to put her to bed she got mad and told me, angrily, to "mind your own beeswax." The sight of her naked white flesh and purplish marks on her legs and arms where she had fallen or banged against the furniture, or something worse, filled me with anger, revulsion, and fear.

After a bender, Mom always had a big hangover; her body trembled, and she would often dispatch me with a note to the hotel saying she had caught the flu and was unable to come to work that day, the same flimsy pretext each time. Then, with gritted teeth, she would begin her gruelling climb back to sobriety, groaning and occasionally bringing up, eating a little, all the while her sheepishness morphing into something more terrible – a sense of guilt that could never be expunged that she had let us all down. My sisters and I were so overjoyed to see her return to her old sober, caring self that her deepening shame did not always register.

Looking back, I marvel at her grit and fortitude for, though she was often down, by dint of her strong will she always managed to bounce back, to issue orders, to set about energetically tidying and cleaning the house, bathing, washing, starching and ironing her white uniform.

For the longest time I was haunted by a recurring nightmare. A man pushes a dinghy from the shore, a woman and three children are sitting in the small boat. He rows the boat toward the middle of a lake. Oars rock in their sockets, fog swirls in pockets, but the man and woman seem oblivious to the danger and start to argue. The children, who have heard it all before, cup their ears. Abruptly, the man declares that he can't take it anymore, dives into the water and starts swimming toward the invisible shore. The woman tells the children not to worry and that she intends to find their Daddy. She strips naked and dives into the water after him and quickly disappears in a grey-blue sulk of fog. The air thickens, night closes in and silence descends. The dark mouth of the lake swallows the children, the dinghy begins to drift.

I wake up from this dream with a scream in my heart.

SO SMOOTH, ALMOST LIKE WATER

Maggie James, our neighbour, began to deteriorate before our eyes. Walking with a cane, she looked weak and worn out, her eyes like blue marbles. I asked Mom what was wrong. She told me about lupus, a tubercular disease of the mucous membranes. "The disease is inside her," she said, "doing its dirty work."

In 1947, Maggie died. For Jack Buller, who had moved across the street into a smaller tenement next to Hin Lee's laundry, Maggie's loss was a crushing blow. He started drinking himself to death.

On top of the usual doldrums of adolescence, I was caught up in my own emotional turbulence. Josh had moved with his family to New York State, making me feel even more isolated. Dad and I had lost each other in the shadow of each other's silences. Dad, another child in the house, never did learn the language of touch. He spurned embraces and other displays of affection. It was as if after his experiences in the war he had built a box and, gathering all his hurts and silences, had curled up inside it like a shivering dog, leaving us to peer through the slats to glimpse his face in blades of light, to listen to the slow shrivelling of his heart.

I began to neglect my schoolwork and my marks plummeted. I spent most of my time at Spiro's Billiard's learning to become a pool "shark." In the grade 10 algebra exam I managed to score a zero, a remarkable feat given that partial marks were awarded even if answers were incorrect. One afternoon in December, just after my birthday, Sister Mary, my grade ten teacher, summoned me to the front of the classroom, and in front of all my snickering classmates told me that I would be better off getting a trade at Canadian General Electric and making something useful of myself rather than wasting the school's time.

"You have as much chance of graduating from high school," she declared in an operatic voice, sweeping the room with her hand till it stopped at the door, "as a chicken has of passing through the eye of that keyhole."

My face crimsoned; I had never been so humiliated in my life. I decided on the spot that lugging dishes as a busboy at the Empress Hotel at 20 cents an hour was preferable to the futility of school. "I quit, Sister," I answered, and marched out of the classroom determined to get a job at the Empress.

One Sunday afternoon when I visited Jack, there was a three-quarter full bottle of Wiser's De Luxe on his coffee table and I asked him if I could have a drink, told him I had never tasted rye before.

"I don't advise it, Jim," he said. "It's powerful medicine." But I kept badgering him until he finally relented and handed me a glass. I immediately poured a drink, tilted my head back and downed it in one prolonged gulp, the way I'd seen Dad do it many times before. It tasted so smooth, almost like water, that I asked for another.

"Take it easy, boy," Jack said. "You're supposed to sip it, not take it straight. You could make yourself sick." But Jack's warnings went unheeded as I kept pouring glass after glass till the bottle was almost drained.

Then the alcohol zapped me like a powerful electric shock: my head exploded, my stomach began to roil and the next thing I knew I was rolling on the floor, sicker than a Greek dog, Jack and the room whirling inside my head. Several hours later, when I finally staggered home across the street and fell into bed, I vaguely remember hearing Dad remark: "He'll be okay, Florie. It'll teach the lad a good lesson." Dad was prophetic: the agony of the three-day hangover was so gut-wrenching that I never touched another drop of rye for fifteen years.

After a few months of schlepping dishes at the Empress Hotel and being patronized and snubbed by some of my former school chums in the cafeteria, I finally decided that the menial sweaty life of a busboy, clearing and lugging dishes for a paltry wage, was not for me. I no longer regarded that job as a destination in life and realized that for too long I'd been rudderless, disoriented and confused. Having come first in grade seven I reckoned I couldn't be academically hopeless, so I decided I'd return to school the following September and try to stop my self-defeating spiral. Thanks to the extra tutoring and encouragement of the nuns, I soon made up for lost ground and even surpassed my classmates. For most of my high-school years I was at or near the top of the class. But my achievements didn't sit well with Dad, who kept hounding me to get "a real man's job" and "start earning your keep," just like he had done at the age of 16. He hectored me to leave school and to apply for a tool-maker's apprenticeship at Canadian General Electric. And later, when I eventually told him that I intended to become a lawyer, he hit the ceiling: "There'll be no crooks in my family, don't expect any help from me!"

Mom became my champion. At night in bed, I would often hear them clashing in the kitchen, Mom berating him for being so negative about my future, Dad arguing it was time I became a "man" in the real world.

"Just because you're a nobody, Sammy," she said, "is no reason for taking it out on the boy. Unlike you, he wants to make something of his life." Though I was still searching for my identity I was determined to succeed. I don't recall Dad ever paying me a compliment, and by the end of high school we rarely spoke. Barry Callaghan in his book *Raise You Five* quotes the French novelist, François Mauriac, who wrote that gambling is a continuous suicide. I believe that Dad's relentless drinking was also a form of slow suicide, a deliberate shutting out of the past and a foreclosure of the future, the only way he knew to cope with the pain of daily living.

His drinking drove a wedge between us, preventing us from expressing our deepest feelings. Hockey alone pierced the emotional gridlock. He would razz me about the Rocket, my hero, always comparing him unfavourably to Gordie Howe. But then, I vividly remember the morning after a playoff game between the Canadiens and Bruins in April 1952. He came upstairs to my bedroom to wake me and announce that the Rocket had scored the winning goal to win the series. He told me how Leo Lebine, the big Bruins defenceman, had checked the Rocket in the second period so hard that he had to be carried off the ice on a stretcher, unconscious, but he'd returned in the third period, bandaged and stitched-up, to score with only four minutes to go. He showed me the *Toronto Star* picture of the Boston goalie, Sugar Henry, his right eye blackened, blood trickling from a gash on his left brow, shaking hands with the Rocket after the game. "I just thought you'd like to know," Dad said, no edge of irony or baiting to his tone. I leapt out of bed, did something I'd never done before. I hugged him hard there in the bedroom.

ALL I WAS TRYING TO DO
WAS TO SAY SOMETHIN' NICE

We had never owned a car and it was long after the war before we got a fridge or a phone. I remember the day our new Frigidaire arrived, how the idea of making her own ice cream thrilled Mom. Dad moved lightly over our lives, scarcely leaving a footprint, but casting a long shadow. Even when he was drinking, however, he would surprise us, like the time he staggered home one Saturday, a small trophy tucked in the crook of his arm, his name on a silver plate identifying him as the winner of the Peterborough Double Cribbage championship.

"How did he do that?" I remember asking Mom after he had tumbled semi-conscious into bed. My remark made her defensive.

"Your dad may be a drinker, son," she said, "but he still has a brain."

As my self-knowledge increased I began to understand what my parents could and could not give. Dad had no gift for fatherhood, or what it meant to be a responsible husband. Yet, they loved each other. Wanted or unwanted, our lives were bound together forever. I couldn't know how not to love them.

Mom continued to fret about Jack Buller's drinking. The last time she had seen him, she said, he looked "all skin and bones." She sent Babe across the street with a ham and cheese sandwich. "Try to make him eat." After rapping on the door and getting no response, Babe turned the handle and swung the door open. A stench like rotten eggs or putrid meat stung her nostrils. Sprawled on his side in the front room, false teeth protruding part way out his mouth, Jack was lying in a pool of blood, a gash on his forehead, his eyes half-open. On the floor near his hand were the brass horses, Moses and Elijah, smeared with blood where he'd struck his head. Babe saw that she was walking in the sticky lake of Jack's blood. She dropped the plate and sandwich, staggered outside, and vomited on the sidewalk.

Mom later told me that Jack had died of cirrhosis of the liver, though the local newspaper had merely reported that his death was the result of a "seizure disorder." I couldn't get the thought of Jack's protruding false teeth out of my mind.

At Lundy's Funeral Home, Jack was laid out in a blue-felt casket. Jack Lundy, the funeral director, Mom, Dad, my two sisters and I, and a handful of others from the lock company were his only mourners. Dad had imbibed before he'd left and during the brief service he started to praise Jack in his robust, room-filling voice, saying what a wonderful neighbour and friend he was, describing his dexterity as a locksmith and the heroism of his volunteer service overseas during the First World War. No one was unduly perturbed until Dad leaned his full weight on one end of the casket and it started to tilt. Jack Lundy pulled Dad away but the casket, which had risen at one end a foot or two, crashed down on the metal gurney. "He's lost a lot of weight, Sam," Jack said. On the way home, Mom ripped into Dad.

"Ah, Florie, all I was trying to do was to say somethin' nice about the man."

OUT TO THE WORLD

In my second last year of high school our football team won the Ontario Catholic Athletic Conference Junior B title, a feat made more remarkable by the size of the team: a mere 14 players at a time when most bigger schools had rosters of 25 or more. We triumphed over the mighty St. Michael's and De La Salle Oaklands of Toronto, and in an exhibition game we defeated our public school archrivals, Peter-bor-ough Collegiate, who historically had trounced us handily. At the end of the season, I was selected for the Best Player Award. Dad grudgingly agreed to attend the father and son banquet at the Kawartha Golf Club where the award cere-mony was being held.

Mom bought Dad a new blue gabardine suit for the occasion. He was partly sloshed before the taxi arrived to take us to the Club.

At the start of the evening, Dad was his "Oirish" self, playing the professional Irishman, twinkly-eyed, charming and loquacious. By dessert time, his eyes were glazed, his words slurry, an unnerving development since he was sup-posed to escort me to the podium for the presentation. Suddenly, just as the speeches got underway, his head pitched forward on the table, cracking a plate, and he was out to the world. Someone phoned a taxi and Dad was taken home, leaving me to a roomful of pitying eyes.

Afterwards, the father of one of my teammates gave me a ride home. "These things happen all the time," he said, but I didn't believe him.

In my senior matriculation year, Mom found a three-bedroom ground-floor duplex on Hunter Street that she loved. It was not far from where we lived, the rent was reasonable and it included a verandah, a small front lawn, a large modern kitchen, a full dining room, a parlour, a fireplace, and shiny maple floors. Mom and I met with the owner of the duplex, Miss Costello, who lived in the other half. She was a pleasant, white-haired retired teacher and wore a gold pendant with a gold cross around her neck. She was clearly impressed that Mom and Dad both had regular jobs and that I would soon be graduating from St. Peter's, her alma mater. We quickly reached an agreement.

"I'm not movin'," Dad roared when we returned to the tenement. "Simcoe Street may not be good enough for you snobs but it's good enough for me."

"We're leaving, Sam," she replied, "whether you're coming or not."

One evening a little later, a neighbour came by to inform us she'd seen Dad sprawled on his back on the Costello's verandah, bellowing in a drunken voice: "Go to hell, all of you. We're not movin'!" Fearful Miss Costello would cancel the lease, Mom and I rushed to the duplex. We discovered that Miss Costello was partially deaf. Once we got home, in her rage Mom shoved Dad onto the bed, yanked down his pants and, as if he were a recalcitrant child, spanked the man of her life hard with the small of her hand.

By 1953, I had waved goodbye to Simcoe Street, had graduated from St. Peter's and had been accepted into the BA programme at McGill. My Aunt Palma had agreed to provide me with a free room in one of her tourist homes not far from the university, and Johnny Lynch, our football coach, had recommended me for a tryout with Vic Obeck, the head coach of the McGill Redman football team.

Dad's "unlived life" had left its thumbprint on me. Son of a man and woman, once young lovers, whose addiction to drink had become self-destructive and deeply disturbing, I was full of determination and ambition, resolved to say "No" to whatever it is that throttles or threatens to throttle the gift of life. I intended to proclaim the all-important "Yes" to those springs of joy that I believed river the heart. More and more I yearned to escape, to make something of my life and not to yield to the siren call of victimhood.

In September of that year, I stood on the platform of the CPR station in Peterborough, hugging and exchanging teary farewells with Mom and my two sisters. At the last moment I spotted Dad floating round the corner of the railway station, legs tottery, jaw fixed and face furrowed like the "No-Surrender Prod" he was, looking as though he was spoiling for one last fight. I waved one final time, turned my back, not in coldness or out of contempt, and quickly boarded the waiting train, bound as it was for the unmet intimate faces of my future.

THIS QUALITY OF MERCY:
EDITING JAMES CLARKE'S POETRY

by Bruce Meyer

This selection has been a labour of love, and, in the process of working on these poems, I learned something about the nature of my own humanity and my need to see the world through the profound sense of empathy that is the hallmark of James Clarke's voice.

I followed his poetry for many years. When I was given the honour to edit this selection, I read and re-read and lived in his books for almost six months. What I think was getting in my way and slowing the project was that I was reading the books front to back. The order of the books was speaking louder than the poems themselves. His volumes often tried to reflect a biographical order with his early life detailed in the opening pages and a temporal flow being reflected in the orchestration of many of the books. In making a book of selected poems for a portion of a larger volume, I had to be certain that the spotlight was on the poems themselves and not merely on events and benchmarks in the life of the poet. Poetry should be more than a memoir, and when a poet's best poems are detached from the poet's biography they inhabit a totally different and unique reality that is larger than the poet himself. My breakthrough in the editorial process came when I decided to read the books back to front, from end to beginning. That's when the order of the original books faded, and the poems, individually, started speaking for themselves. That is when something beautiful at the core of James Clarke's work emerged. It was the voice of mercy.

Many years ago when I was going through a difficult portion of my own life and doubting my ability to move beyond the trials and tribulations of the moment, James Clarke spoke to me several times a week. During our telephone conversations I realized that he was more than a judiciary figure or even a poet: he was someone who in his own life, through tremendous suffering, had achieved that rare kind of clarity that comes only through the power to hold tenaciously to empathy. Here was a mind that did not simply judge: it examined life and sought life through the power of humane critical judgment.

The story that emerges from this entire volume of poems and memoirs and tributes is that of a man who has had to face enormous suffering but who has learned so much in the process. His understanding is something he has shared in his poetry as each poem investigates, tests, challenges and responds to the pain he has had to endure. But rather than crying or crying uncle, Clarke's poetry achieves that most valuable element that all too rarely arises from the depths of suffering and tragedy: understanding. To suffer is to be human. To learn from suffering and share that learning with others is to be the most important kind of poet we can encounter in the art of the written word.

To honour the poet and the all-too-easily-overlooked revisitations of the necessity of love and dignity and empathy and mercy and wisdom that reside at the core of Clarke's work, I chose the best poems not merely for the stories they told, but for the truths they contained. I have tried to order them so that they resonate off each other — not an explanatory order or an imposed biographical sequencing, but a structure that tells a story (of sorts) without imposing a story on the poems themselves.

In reading Clarke's work, I realized two key things. The first is that he is far more than a judge: he is a brilliant poet who knows how to harness powerful ideas that seldom come easily or without great cost. That had to be my prime concern, namely, to showcase his work as a poet and to make the poems jump off the page so that the entire book would be a page-turner. My second realization was that (alas) the judge poems were only a small aspect of the soul behind the poems. I have tried to let that soul (not the man on the bench or the learned spokesman for the ironies of the law) tell its own story and speak for itself. Clarke continually reminds us that there is a higher law and that its voice has to be heard.

James Clarke's best poems have an aura of holiness about them, a voice of hard-won knowledge, a contemplative directness, and an air of narrative and conversational prayer that is psalm-like. I think this is what Lorca may have meant in his essay "On the Theory and Function of the Duende." Some of the poems achieve that sense of the wry wit that has been his poetic hallmark for the past twenty years, but the great success of his work is not just wry wit, but the soul and the spirit behind a life that has, in an uneasy and sometimes tenuous way, understood that judging is not the imposition of the law in a clinical fashion, but the art of learning about the self and surviving the life of the self through the powerful grace of living life as an expression of mercy. The prime organizing principle in this selection *is* the voice of mercy, and I hope I have brought that to the fore. These poems are a moving statement about how the poet remands us to the custody of our own humanity.

SELECTED POEMS

Palm-in-the-Hand Story

One evening a gang of murderers & thieves
came to the monastery at Assisi seeking
food & lodging—Francis was away, preaching
in a nearby village. When Brother Antonio

unbolted the door & observed their unsavoury
looks, he panicked, told them the monastery was
full. After Francis returned next day & learned what
had happened he called his followers together.

"Everyone's our brother & sister," he told them.
Then he instructed Antonio to find the outcasts
& bring them back to the monastery so they could
make amends. When Antonio found the gang

camped in a field not far from the monastery he
was filled with remorse. He knelt on the ground
before them, bowed his head & begged for
forgiveness. In one clean blunt stroke his head

went flying through the air like an ear of corn.
The gang stripped his tunic, left his naked body
in the field & sent his severed head back to the
monastery in a stolen oxcart. When Francis saw

the beatific look on Antonio's face, he lifted eyes
to heaven in thanksgiving, praised God for
his infinite mercies.

Villanelle

The best years are the first to go,
they vanish with the summer green;
old age always lingers slow.

The harvest fields soon fill with snow
& all the stately trees between;
the best years are the first to go.

Fluted bone that the wind blows
whistles like a frosted screen;
old age always lingers slow.

When I was young I didn't know
days were numbered or how, unseen,
our sun is always first to go.

I watched my first love go
before her season; now autumn, lean
& chill is here & conspires slow

to kill my roses row on row
& choke my silent scream;
the best years are the first to go,
old age always lingers so.

The Steeple
(for Father Kevin)

I climbed to the top
     of the old stone church,
sneaked up the staircase
     to the choir loft, ascended
the ladder to the windy belfry;
     steeple swayed,
splinters scratched my face,
     nails tore my clothes
as I groped skyward
     into that narrowing space,
darkness round me closing
     like a trap,
fearful, perhaps I had gone too far,
     till at last I bumped my head
against the Cross,
     discovered I had no place else to turn.

Heart's Needle

Last evening

as darkness thickened I walked down to the
lake to listen to the

thrum of raindrops, watch the ripples flatten &
fade, a break of moonlight

on the darkish sand. Slowly, slowly
I am learning to unclench my fist.

Judge's Prayer

What pardon for this, Lord?
All my life I pursued Reasonable Doubt,
clung to her like a drowning sailor
to a raft at sea,
did not always follow your command
to smite the wicked,

        set the innocent free.

I doubted, Lord, & I doubted, Lord, till
my mind grew grey. Forgot your way, Lord.
More than your certitudes Lord I loved
the shifting shape of reason—
its enthralments & futilities, shovelled
clouds of words into the wide mouth of doubt,

        eschewed prejudice & sympathy,
danced like a besotted lover
on the cool blue pinhead of logic
till the legs within my legs gave out, all
passion spent.

What pardon for this, Lord: just lawgiver,
harbour & master?
I plead guilty, deserve
to be punished.

The Quality of Mercy

The highest work of God is mercy.
    —ECKHART

During sentencing, the judge
was distracted by a housefly

buzzing in his ears & mizzling
over his eyelids & cheeks. Distracted,

he could think of little but
how to rid himself of his tormentor.

After several near misses he swatted
the fly & as it lay squirming,

stunned & helpless, he plucked
antennae, wings & one by one

six hairy jointed legs. Only when the
fly was disabled—a greenish metallic nub—

did he look up,
bits of wings stuck to his

fingers, in time to catch
counsel begging "the mercy of the court."

Last Caravan to Damascus

(for Gay & Graham)

A singularly bleak December it was,
cold, icy, our bodies flaring in the winter
moonlight; we cut a deal with the police,

but planned a different route; we all knew
the importance of a good story. Marauding
bands of zealots almost did us in, forced us

to detour around their camps. When I dropped
out at the Temple to buy bagels & a teddy
bear the others went on ahead with the baskets

of gifts; I scrambled to catch up but never saw
them again. No star shone in the darkness;
no sleigh bells jingled in

the air. The evening turned out more bodiless
than I ever dared imagine. By the time
I found the hostel—a rude & drafty barn, shocked

to see the press already there—the family had
fled, vanished beasts & all without a trace, no
forwarding address. I was disappointed to say

the least; missed connections are the story
of my life. Humiliated too; the shepherds
snickered behind my back. I gave the bagels &

teddy bear to street kids, what else to do?
Left that hostile land as ceremoniously as I could,
caught the last caravan to Damascus.

But despite my disappointment a voice
inside my heart kept whispering not to fret,
the family was happy & unharmed. Now

years later, many bizarre & terrible things
have come to pass—too numerous to relate;
but when I think of that freezing barn

I still regret I came too late, never
saw the child, feel a twinge of pity for
the young man who was me, a callow

adventurer in a strange country, benighted &
alone, without a map, no one to thank,
no gifts to unwrap.

The Scary Thing

is you can say anything:

that the diamond solitaire just below the place
you love to be kissed will slow your breathing;

that all you need for happiness is an island where
the pulse slows in time to the undulating waves &
you can hear the song of the kiskadee miles away;

that those shiny appliances will take the frazzle
out of your marriage;

that the revolutionary skin serum with 8% Mexican yam will
soothe the torrential inner sanctum of your body & give you peace;

that this new seductive perfume will make you drop your
broom & raise hell;

that the line between sensuality & safety no longer
exists in your automobile;

that your garden will be the talk of the beehive,

& someone will believe you.

Act of Mercy

She was convinced toothpaste had infested the house.
Gobs of it kept appearing on floor, sofa, coffee table,

beds, children's clothing, everywhere, even in the food.
She spent days scrubbing floors, scouring pots & pans,

disinfecting walls; she complained of canker
sores, headaches, abdominal pains. But when she told

her husband, he said she should see a shrink.
The woman from the Health Department, who inspected

the house & found nothing, said it was all in
her head. The manufacturer sent her a list of the

ingredients, all non-toxic, disclaimed responsibility.
Her psychiatrist diagnosed depression, prescribed

Paxil. She persuaded her husband to move finally
—they looked at dozens of houses—but the virus,

as she called it, always followed her. When the children
began to complain of nightmares, nausea & other pains,

she told neighbours the virus had penetrated
their skin, was eating their intestines & would

eventually pop out their eyes & kill them. She couldn't
sleep, began to see flashing lights. She felt

isolated, misunderstood, trapped in a house of horror.
At her trial, she testified she had no choice.

What mother could allow her children to suffer?

Chekhov's Journey

On the Siberian steppes on the last leg
of a journey of ten thousand versts, he
travelled in a contraption no bigger
than a cart, a tumbledown

tarantass harnessed to two horses, drawn
by an old coachman—a "wicker basket"
he called it—twelve days of torture
over rutted roads, each jolt

a hammer in his back. As he observed
the passing milestones, puddles, birch
stands, the flat fields & log & sod huts
crowded with settlers, convicts, bums,

all the dumb & patient misery of humanity
sifted through his bones, cut like the cold
blade of wind that chafed his cheeks, pried
open his new leather overcoat; he saw

himself as a goldfinch in a cage peering
through bars at the harsh "once only"
in which we breathe & cast our shadow—
a clear, unshuttered gaze, a God's eye,

seeing everything, forgetting nothing.

Great Blue Heron

(for Bruce)

All day the hunter watched
as snow fell over lake & wood;
when sky emptied

its big, silk purse coins lay
scattered across the heaven;
& the hunter slept, dreaming

he was a great blue heron. And while
he dreamt, three deer
stood on the snowy

lake gazing at the night;
& for a few moments the night held
handfuls of silver, the dreaming

hunter, & the three deer,
soft eyes impaled
by Orion's bright spears;

& when the hunter woke
only the windprints of the wings
remained.

Please Write Soon

I love letters spun from the transparent
fibres of the heart: nothing stimulates

me more than the flutter of mail pushing
through the slot like moths. I

keep them close at hand, the way a flamenco
dancer holds a fan, change continents

just to fondle their delicate frames. Today
alas, bills, notices, circulars by the

score, but letters scarcely anymore,
faded like ghostly silhouettes on

a darkened screen; even letters to get
letters are of no avail; intimacy travels

so swiftly these days my news is always
stale; friends tell me when I complain

that I must get e-mail. O for the bloom
of handwriting on a page—the porous

human smudge! A perfect printout is never
quite the same. Please write soon.

The Quarry

(for Monsignor Newstead)

I'm a trader, not a philosopher. I pay
my taxes, keep my camels fed;
religion does not engage my better self
or interest me.

Not that I have much faith in the goat
of humanity. Once in Damascus
I witnessed the police chop off the hand
of a boy for stealing figs. In the passes

I've come across brigands lashed to rocks,
left for the vultures' meal. I've learned it's best
to look the other way, keep the lips
sealed. What then made me stop?

I heard the shouts, glimpsed the woman
kneeling in the dust, the upraised stones
like fists of gold; I saw him step
forward, talk to them,

then write with finger on the ground.
One by one, starting with the elders,
they threw down their stones, drifted off,
till there was no one left but me.

How to Bribe a Judge

Snap to attention when he enters the
courtroom & never fail to say:
"GOOD MORNING."

Smile—make him feel welcome as a lover.

Laugh heartily at all his jokes even when
they're incomprehensible.

When he says something particularly absurd
chime in: "I wish I'd thought of that."

Ponder deeply—learn the art of furrowing the
brow or staring gravely at the ceiling—
especially when he's talking silly.

Without appearing obsequious finish every
sentence with "My Lord."

Quote with boldness from his old decisions,
no matter how dull, irrelevant or wrong.

When he's patently confused, interject:
"Would you mind repeating that, My Lord,
I missed the subtlety of it." Or try a
variation: "You're one step ahead of me
as usual, My Lord."

Tell him his judgments are novel, break
new ground. Avoid meretricious adjectives
like "brilliant"; he'll know it's flattery.

Send him a Christmas card, expressing
gratitude for his birth.

Never offer cash—his dignity will be
slighted.

Finally, never appeal his judgments.

The author recites "How to Bribe a Judge" ~ 2:14
www.tinyurl.com/KidSimcoeStreet-ReadingPoem

Slow Waltz   4

Don't blame me if I waltz slower,
the hand is reeling round the clock;
we'll all go down to the field together.

There's barely breath to smell the clover
before our little dance is over;
don't blame me if I waltz slower.

When I was younger I cried "faster, faster"
& yearned to whirl instead of walk;
we'll all go down to the field together.

Numbly I watched my first love falter
& blow away like a puff of chalk;
don't blame me if I waltz slower.

Too soon I heard the ploughman shudder,
too late I glimpsed the darkening rock;
we'll all go down to the field together.

Acres of salt ponds I've spilt to recover
the heart's still centre; so don't mock
or blame me if I waltz slower;
we'll all go down to the field together.

A Judge's Progress

At the beginning he wrote judgments
to follow the Law
& please the Court of Appeal.

When the Court of Appeal disagreed
he knew
he was doing something wrong.

At the end he wrote judgments
to please himself
& follow the Court of Conscience.

When the Court of Appeal disagreed
he knew
he was doing something right.

A Sad Tale

The old judge woke one morning,
>   bedsheets rumpled,
>   chest cracked open like a husk,
>   gasping for air.

Instantly he knew the thing
>   he dreaded most—the occupational
>   hazard his colleagues talked about
>   had happened:

his heart had flown, sprung from its rib cage
>   without a trace
>   in the dead of night while he
>   lay dreaming

of the wheel of perfect justice.
>   A note dangling from the bedroom door:
>   *After years of neglect,* the heart said,
>   *I can't take it any more.*

Satori in Surin

The old monk led me
into the inner courtyard;
above us perched the

Buddha on his lacquered
dais—a golden pear.
Doves burbled on the

ivied walls, fragrance
of jasmine filled the air, a
breeze ruffled the skin

of the pool. The old monk
clasped my hand; the pool
rilled with tiny suns;

I thought I heard the tinkle
of bells from far away. There
was a breath of wings, a

tremble of light as though
a dark bird had flown
from my brow. Something

happened; I do not know.

The Mingling

That spring morning after Benoît,
one of the young residents at L'Arche,
choked to death in his sleep
(he'd had an epileptic seizure)
I met Père Thomas, swishing
to chapel along the Rue Principale
clad in his long, loose Dominican
habit, the pale sun shining
on his pâte. "Too bad about Benoît,"
I said. He glanced at me kindly,
lifted his pale blue eyes
to the sky & said, almost as if I'd
missed the point: "Benoît
is now with the Father in Heaven."
Then he smiled & added:
"Death's our real birthday."

A short time after your death
when I told a visiting priest
from Sri Lanka that you'd leapt
to your drowning at Niagara,
he said, eyes suddenly aglow:
"Wow, imagine being swept
into the arms of Jesus, it takes
my breath away." His voice rose
as he urged me to make a retreat

at the Carmelite monastery.
"Let your prayers mingle
with the mighty waters," he said.

Ode to the Passenger Pigeon

(Ectopistis Migratorius)

*On September 1st, 1914, Martha, the last passenger
pigeon, died in a Cincinnati zoo.*

I'd like to have been there in spring when
      you flocked to the Saugeen, thicker
than the green hair of earth,
      your sleek, pointed wings & long, slender tail
darkening the air.

I'd like to have heard the threshing
      of your wings passing overhead
like a hard gale at sea or
      the deep, booming basso of Niagara.

I wish I could have gazed
      at your iridescent feathers,
amazed at the flickering greens & purples
      in changing light, a streamer
of shot silk unravelling the noonday sun &

visited your rookeries,
      a white longhouse strung for miles
across woods & fields of Amabel & Albemarle
      as far north as the lands of the Ojibwa,
trees uprooted by the weight
      of your landings.

Oh how I wish I could have been part of
          your journeyings,
held your frail bones
          gently in my hands,
cupped the feathered softness
of your beating heart
just once.

Prayer for Travellers

Father, look kindly on those doomed to travel the earth,
taking photographs, mailing postcards, buying made-in-

Taiwan souvenirs, & walking around in drip-dry nylon
underwear. Give them wisdom in the selection of

hotels, that they may find their reservations honoured &
hot water running in the taps. We pray that the telephone

works, the operator speaks English & that e-mail is
available. Lead them to inexpensive restaurants where

the food is superb, the waiter friendly & the wine
complimentary. Light their paths with sunshine & photo

opportunities & spare them the affliction of dogs, horses,
& fellow-travelling bores. Forgive, too, their inability

to tip. Make the locals love them for who they are,
not what they can do for the economy. Grant them

the stamina to visit museums, cathedrals, national
parks, colonial houses, convict jails, no matter

how depressing, dull & dreary. And if, perchance,
they should falter & fail to see

an historic site in order to nap after lunch, have mercy
on their willing, but weak flesh. AMEN.

Death Row

I lived on death row
when I was small,
never knew if
I would live or die.

I shuddered
when I heard their boots
pounding down the hall
the same hour Friday nights.

I never knew my fate
until the peephole clanged,
& I
smelled the beery stench,
saw the glassy eye.

The black current
twisted through my mind
but they always brought me back to life,
told me I would never get reprieved,
that Friday nights go on forever.

Palma Has Beautiful Dahlias

When Minoune, Palma's old yellow cat, was ready to give birth, she settled into the wood box Palma had fixed up on the screen porch and rolled over on her side like she was about to nap. Everything happened in slow motion. Minoune braced herself against the side of the box and pushed. As the shiny sacs slid out Minoune pounced on the umbilical cord. The cord was tough as old leather and it took Minoune a long time to chew through. Each newborn opened its mouth and gulped, legs pawing the air, and began to suckle, paying no heed to its brothers and sisters. By the end of the afternoon a mass of breathing fur clung to the mother's belly. Then Minoune licked her mouth with her pink tongue and laid her forepaw across her brood. I watched as Palma punched holes in the bottom of a large margarine container and filled a yellow pail with lukewarm water. Then she took Minoune outside, where she scratched at the screen, trying to get back in. One at a time Palma lifted the babies from the box and laid them gently in the margarine container. Their squeals sounded like distant seagulls. Palma placed the lid on the container and put a small stone on top. I always say a little prayer before I do this, she said. She lowered the container into the yellow pail. As she descended the stairs to the basement the squeals grew louder. Halfway down Palma glanced back. After they're dead, I bury them in my garden, she said. Palma has beautiful dahlias.

The River

After court the judges go down to the river.

They shed their sashes, their silk robes.

Stand on the shore naked.

Dip their pale swollen feet in the water.

The river moves quietly.

The judges breathe in great gulps of clean air.

The first thing they do is wash the blood from their hands.

Home

Not anymore the steep edge
of the field, the wet sedge,

not anymore the pins of light in
polar night;

I have fitted my hand to the latch,
the sloping roof, found

that haven in the mind where
kisses, bread, talk

are cradled, the gravity of the
world lifted,

a place to hold onto against
the long hours of emptiness,

the irremediable cold.

Minnows

All the eyewitnesses agreed
that the day of the accident
was warm & sunny.

The victim testified that
she entered the intersection
on a green light & the accused
struck the front of her car.

The accused testified that
he entered the intersection
on a green light & the victim
struck the front of his car.

The old lady rocking
on the verandah testified
that the accused definitely
ran the red light.

The young man on the Suzuki motorcycle
testified that the accused
definitely stopped
at the red light.

The pensioner strolling on the sidewalk
testified that everything happened so fast
he couldn't say what colour the light was.

The judge remembered another golden day
at Jackson's Creek & the minnows
that kept shimmering past

his small, awkward hands.

The Mystical Foundation of Authority

The reverse side also has a reverse side.
—Japanese proverb

For years the judge loved the interplay
of language & logic, saw them as tools
to probe the real world, discover "the truth
the whole truth & nothing but the truth,"

until, that is, he studied linguistics &
learned from Wittgenstein that reality's
a figment of the mind, true & false,
social artifacts & all law—a matter of politics.

Now, on wet autumn evenings he drifts
about his house looking for dustballs, leans
against the gloomy furniture, ponders the dialects
of rain, the bat-squeaks in the walls,

the strange collusion of it all.

Relic

The last I saw of her alive
she was in bed; she blew
a kiss, waved farewell, she'd
see me when I got back, she said.

Almost ten years to the day as I
rummaged in our dresser drawers
preparing for a holiday, a perfume
bottle—amber, the colour

of her hair—poked up from under
a mound of socks & underwear,
fluted, hard, like an ancestral bone
breaking through the sod, or

a dark shell you'd find upon
a beach, ground round & smooth &
bare by the scraping of the sea, a relic
from another world, empty of all

being, the long ocean in between.

Variations

I

I overhear my old aunt on the phone say:
"I feel badly," & then hang up, hobble back

to the table to tell me Arthur has passed away.
A stroke at 84. Arthur was her

second husband; they were married 11 years,
divorced two years ago.

Then her eyes wander back to the Scrabble
board. "Whose turn is it?" she said.

II

My daughter, who's pregnant with her
first child, drops by for a visit. She's

expecting a millennium-day baby: "I've hired
a doula for emotional support," she says.

"Why not? In this life you only get one turn."

III

Later that evening when we are alone
my aunt slumps in her armchair

in the living room, stares into space for
the longest while. "He came here a month

ago to pick up the last of his things,
you know," she says, "told me he still

loved me." Then she looks at me, tears
in her eyes: "I guess my turn's next."

Angel of Justice

Coaxing her to fly is never easy.
Mostly she's content to perch beside

me on the bench—a skinny angel
with wooden wings—play dumb

or press her eyelids closed, pretend
that she's asleep. Sometimes to get

her attention I tickle her dainty
feet or croon a ditty in her ear,

but she always feigns indifference,
lets on she doesn't hear or care.

Then just when you're tempted to put
her blindfold back & give her

up for dead she startles everyone—
lawyers, litigants, reporters—all

the jaded crowd—by quickening back
to life, flaps her creaky hinges &

like the phoenix from the fire, soars
blueward in a blinding

rush of wings, higher & higher up
the corridors of air, till at last

she rings the halo of the sun.

What the Judge Failed to Mention

In sentencing the young man to the penitentiary
the judge said he hoped he'd learned that
crime doesn't pay.

The judge failed to mention all the
other lessons the young man would learn
in that granite underworld

where love belongs to a lost language
& everyone drinks from the wormwood cup,

where you wake to a sullen sky
wondering where the light of the world has fled.

Tribal Customs

(for Justice Speyer)

Lawyers love to beat dead horses;
when the horse won't move they

buy stronger whips, change riders.
Sometimes the government appoints

a committee to visit race tracks,
stables, paddocks, clubhouses—

all the favourite watering holes.
Invariably the committee will

set new standards for riding &
recommend that no one dismount,

which leads to the present
craze—a phenomenon that never

ceases to amaze—lawyers proud
in the saddle like Gary Cooper,

astride several dead horses harnessed
together for greater speed,

prancing on the same spot repeatedly
& going nowhere in a great hurry.

Twentieth-Century Love Song

I

Behold, my Lord comes,
earlobes glistening with rhinestones,
body sweeter than nard.

Like a stag he bounds
across the boulevards of the city
dodging parked cars,

leaping over shoppers, his voice
a column of smoke, blowing
my name.

The one I sought among the hinds
of the field has found me,
knocks on my door, speaks to me.

II

Come, Daughter of Toronto,
winter is past,
hie with me over the mountain

into the Valley of Lovecraft,
throw away your Birkenstocks,
put on your stilettos;

let us taste together the secret
potions of the love merchant,
saunter hand in hand

down the bright aisles stacked high
with G-strings & lingerie,
feather boas & jock harnesses;

blindfolded, let us romp among
the cockrings & ball stretchers,
lay our drowsy heads

on lovemats, strewn with silicone
dildos & neon condoms;
make haste, my love,

fondle me with full-flavoured
unguents from Paris, rub me
with scented oils from California;

let me manacle your wrists
with leather tongs, bind your ankles
with padded chains,

for you are beautiful, my love,
my lily among brambles, & I
am sick with love.

Night Execution

The darkness around me is deep
as I listen to him scrabbling

in the wall, nuzzling
for crumbs or a nest to rest

his head. I find it hard to
ignore his presence, get some

sleep, but when I hear the jaws
snap shut, the scraping on

the floor, I spring awake, switch
on the lamp, remove the panel

behind the door, beam my flashlight
in. The trap (two for one

at the Dollar Store) is
tilted on its side, the brass bar

that promised instant death
missed the neck, fell across

the spine instead. I pull on yellow
rubber gloves, reach inside &

bring him out, alive—a rag toy—
crushed in two with

big, imploring eyes; I hesitate,
but only for a second

—his back is broken, he cannot
live. I must do what I must do,

then rush to wash my hands
& back to sleep.

How to Build a Modern Bird House

Decide what species you want.
Measure the entrance
with care; neither big enough

for predators nor small enough
to ruffle feathers. Assemble
your tools: handsaw, claw hammer,

screwdriver & drill.
Keep the saw well honed,
cut with a steady eye.

Make slits for drainage &
ventilation; a bird should feel
part of earth & sky

not a prisoner in his own
castle. Finally, hang the
birdhouse near shrubs &

trees, where birds like to
nest. Remember, a house
cobbled together

cannot last. Hammer
love between your nails.

The Way Everyone Is Inside

What are you doing with your life?
This is a good Buddhist question.
You didn't buy it.
It's quite sobering, but the way
the world is being organized, bigger parts
of it are sliding inexorably into
smaller, where we live,
we don't even know we're being bruised.

When the raging elephant (or angry
boss, it makes no difference) comes charging
it's already too late.

The old millennium is darkening like a window,
the bus is breaking down:
ball bearings have sprung loose, we're desperately
in need of a cosmic catching mitt—a fresh way
of seeing;
a new sun's begging to be born.

Permanence

(for Amelia)

After the funeral my granddaughter whispered in her
mother's ear: "I want to be alone with Papa," &
so I took her by the hand, led
her into the living room, thinking
we could have a quiet time together.
She leaned the slight weight
of her four-year-old head against my chest, nestled
in my arms, mute & still & safe &

for the longest while we held each other—our
hearts, two shells resonating in the dark—
the wet, white seconds like lanterns soaking up
the night, her life-breath—a small urgent bell
making me promise over & over I would never leave.

While you were sleeping

a crazy thing happened: your wife
got up from the sofa,
      left for the corner store
to buy a pack of cigarettes
        & never came back.

For years she's been seen
      wandering in suburbia,
pounding on doors,
      begging for tenderness.

Recently midnight strollers
      have reported sightings
of her,
      larger than life,
sleepwalking
      toward the moon,
shouting your name.

"How-to"

books on wellness proliferate,

how to prevent:
    Alzheimer's
    strokes
    heart disease
    the big C,

how to manage:
    eating disorders
    glaucoma
    menopause
    stress,

how to treat:
    the vulnerable hip
    the frozen shoulder
    creaky joints
    incontinence, etc. etc.

There are even manuals on how
    to resuscitate
    your fingernails & toes.

Libraries galore, in brief, on how
to cheat the End, but

nothing to show you
what to live for.

Silver Mercies

"It takes seven years for a suicide,"
the priest said, but I was too numb

to hear his words: that was the black
spring tongues of tulips pierced my

heart & the thought of never seeing
her again was more than I could bear.

Last night when her long beautiful
arms reached across the bed, huge with

desire, & I could not even remember her
voice, that rich resonance that once filled

our home with warmth & joy, 1 grieved for
all our faithless flesh too small for

even strongest love; but snow,
our comforter, knows us better than

ourselves & covers us whitely, seven
times seven, with soft forgetfulness, &

just as the hibiscus never completely fades
but rises red & radiant always

in our mind, so too the snowy voices
of those we loved live on in our reborning

selves, silver mercies of the dead.

The Fire

In the dream he walked across a field
under the palest, silken blue, past

the tall sweet corn, all the way to
the big pond where he dug a trench, circled

it with rocks, gathered bark, wood shavings,
twigs, coniferous seed cones, dead

wood, branches for fuel; then, as dusk
descended & fireflies came out he

built a pyre that lit up pond & sky, &
wife, child, mother, father, sister, grand-

parents, relatives, old friends, none dead,
none absent, joined him at the fire,

dark faces polished with love, no one
speaking, as though everyone was seeing

each other for the first time, shriven &
accepted as they'd always dreamed, eyes

picked clean by the long patience of death.

Dreamworks (1990)

I

We're driving across the Arizona desert.
Suddenly a storm blows up, sticks,

sand, tumbleweeds bounce across
the pavement, a tumbleweed

snags on the bumper like a burr. We decide
to stop the van, wait out

the storm. I want to have sex but
she isn't interested. Now the wind

picks up, leans on the van, shakes
it like a toy. Outside everything

is bathed in eerie, yellow light, a nether
world between life & death.

II

I search for the wedding
ring: under the bed, the closet, the cabinet

in the washroom—even the rumpled bedclothes—
but it's nowhere to be found. I can't even

remember what it looks like. When the nurse
comes in we go through the dresser drawers

together: an old nightgown (the top torn),
a pair of soiled white gloves, one onyx earring,

a broken rosary, her Bulova watch still ticking,
a brush with three loops of red hair, a journal,

some entries torn out, but no ring.
I wonder if someone has stolen it.

III

I see her coming down the centre aisle of
the church; she's smiling & in a rush as

usual, dressed in yellows, duns, russet
reds, the colours of autumn, her

favourite season. I wave but she
pretends not to notice. Suddenly it

strikes me that I've been the victim of
a black joke, that she faked everything,

& knew all long that sooner or later
I'd find out.

IV

Smoke engulfs the motel. The children
are inside but it's too late, heat

singes my skin, flames shimmy
up the walls. She bolts toward the

entrance—I grab her sleeve but she breaks
free, dives into the tumbling inferno. The last

I see of her, she's running across a window,
hair on fire, a child in her arms.

V

I swim in the cold grotto of memory,
past the flotsam, the wavering eel grass,

the silver schools of mackerel, my eyes
a pair of phosphorescent fish, starlight

thrumming off my shiny scales, thinking
of her, searching for her hiding place

in the shadowy weeds.

Thin Man

(a circus story)

On April 1st, 1928 Calvin Sprague, the original
Thin Man, married Bunny, the Fat Lady.

For eight years they'd kept company in circuses,
on the stage & at Coney Island where they did

a dance act together, sharing the sideshow platform
with Freddie the Armless Fiddler, Flo the Elastic

Plastic Squaw & Felix the Frogman. Look!
there's Calvin thin as a flattened straw beside his bride,

with high hat, morning coat, winged collar &
white gloves, carrying a silver-headed cane. People

claimed his skin was so tight you could see his
milk-stick bones, watch his heart tick. Bunny's

favourite dish was pumpkin pie & whipped cream
which she had every day, but Calvin's diet

was another matter:—a little wine & steamed rice.
Bunny loved to joke she liked her lovers "paper thin."

When she passed away in 1938—a case of acute food poisoning—Calvin was devastated.

"After her death," he told reporters years later, "my life never returned to normal."

Judges

Not birds of paradise
coo-cooing in their golden crests,

or randy crows
cawing on hot pavements,

but emperor penguins,
who never waddle

from their rookeries.
Even the white plumes

of humpbacks on the horizon
can't nudge them

from their closed circles

Revenant

Woke up suddenly—a nightshift
of crickets outside our bedroom
window, thinking
—only for the briefest second—
you were there beside me on the bed &
I could breathe your breath in the blue night
air, deeply, slowly,

reached across the sheets to touch
your cheek—stopped, remembered;
the moonlight on your pillow cold.

Most of the time

you don't need a crystal ball
to know exactly where you
intend to go even before the
case is over.
But after a close custody battle
or when you have to sentence
a first offender,
you leave the courtroom,
your mind a blizzard,
wondering how you'll ever
find a way
through that whiteness.

Ice Storm

Early this morning
a bohemia of glass
outside the sunroom;

me, breathless,
a stranger
in my own country

Report from the Judicial System to the Public

He was an only child & did all the normal things
for a boy his age. Cubs. Scouts. Church league

hockey. Neighbors remarked on his easy smile and
winsome ways. He loved rock concerts and music videos,

wore baggy pants and expensive sneakers. In high
school he moved with the right crowd

& was popular with the girls. At 14 he started to
smoke grass & drink. He screwed up at school.

He never forgave his father for once hitting him
when he came home drunk. He resented his mother

for always being on his case. Three days before
Christmas & two days after his 17th birthday

he came home one evening with a loaded semi-automatic
.22 & pumped four bullets into each

of their skulls. Afterwards, he treated himself
to a steak dinner downtown with his mom's pin money

before reporting the killings to the police. He
is called a Young Offender, still a teenager with

big, awkward hands & embarrassing zits.
The shrinks will try to figure out what went wrong.

In three years he will be delivered back to you.

Don Juan *en Repos*

After years in hot pursuit of the hooded
clitoris he's decided to give his aging

bedroom eyes a rest, retire to a secluded
Barbadian beach where every evening

the sun spreads its gold fan across the
waning of desire, makes him forget the

lint & litter of the uncommitted life, the
sweet suck of coupling molecules, the

little steaming signatures of self he'd left
behind. No more hugs & kisses, no more

sweaty, panting trysts, gone forever reveries
of the perfect thigh & breast, the fabled

crotch. Whole mountainsides could slide
loosening with desire & he wouldn't bat

an eye; even those bronzed, red-lipped
beauties on the sand, slathering oil

on leggy limbs, can't make him change
his mind. "I don't need romantic fixes

any more," he says, sinking on his solitary
bed like a castaway in the deep. A blue

indifference, like hypothermia, has settled
in. Now he steeps himself in the nocturnal

nectar of orchids & bougainvillea getting
in shape for the afterlife, satisfied—such is

his heart's new calm—to listen to the slurry
mantra of the surf, let the cool sea air

run its long chaste fingers through his
thinning hair, contemplate the lacquered

jewel box of the night, the Sea of Tranquillity
on the ostrich-egg moon, swoon like Morpheus

into the feathered arms of sleep.

Going Home

Be patient.
We are going home.
It is not far. We are rocking
in the great belly of the ship.
No light cracks the dark sea, but
the ship is strong, the voyage
will not be long.

We will arrive early.
It will be morning. We will
rub our unshelled eyes, see
the shore rise.
We will untangle our bones & play
in the lemon groves, dwell
in a white house near blue water.
There will be time. Be patient.
We are going home.

Shamanic Cure for a Dry-Souled Judge

Remove his robe & the fine dressings of civility,
    bury him naked in the New Mexican desert.

Plant a parasol in the sand to shade him from
    the sun, stop the nimble sentences springing

from his tongue. Tell him he'll have to overcome
    his dread of scorpions & snakes, shed his skin

of aloof dispassion. Let him nibble on the hard crust
    of loneliness & pain, hear again the lovebeat of the

heart, thirst for laws never given birth. Read him
    long lists of cheerless cases till words collapse &

blown into darkness his shell begins to crack,
    explodes with grief at the burning roof of earth.

Sunset

Another evening drawing in
across the lake as we gather
by the window to see the spent
sun burning deep inside the
trees, cottage wall aflame.
Compassed by doubt & dark I
try to cup the dancing fire.
"Shame it doesn't stay," I say,

forgetting in my heart's desire
that someone, somewhere on this
turning globe, is always catching
gold, the dazzling coin spinning
from eye to eye, the air beyond
our darkening hands holier than rain.

Kiss me

if you must, dear,
but it won't do

much good; December
is here

& I'm too cold;
I should have been

kissed months ago
when blossoms

grazed the lips of
May; now kisses

only stir dead leaves,
make me

feel old & dry,
wondering where

the rains were when
I was young.

photograph by Mark Tearle

PUBLISHED WORKS

L'Arche Journal (1973)

Silver Mercies (1997)

The Raggedy Parade (1998)

The Ancient Pedigree of Plums (1999)

The Way Everyone Is Inside (2000)

Flying Home Through the Dark (2001)

How to Bribe a Judge (2002)

Forced Passage (2005)

A Mourner's Kaddish (2006)

Dreamworks (2008)

Left to right, top to bottom:

Babe, James and Shirl on his new bike in front of the tenement.

Mom as a young woman.

Dad with two fellow soldiers, taken in England.

James and sisters atop a woodpile; the Peterborough fire hall in background.

Mom and Dad before he was sent overseas.

Dad as a young man in his Bellhop uniform.

Mom and James at Jackson's Creek.

Mom and James' sisters in front of the tenement.

Dad in his military uniform.

James in the backyard; Jack's cat in background.

"The new fire hall mascot." James behind the wheel of the local fire truck.

Mom (left) and Gabby, behind the fire hall.

James on the fire hall's wire fence.